ALSO BY PAUL CARTER

Don't Tell Mum I Work on the Rigs,
She Thinks I'm a Piano Player in a Whorehouse

This Is Not a Drill

Is That Thing Diesel?

RIDE LIKE HELL AND YOU'LL GET THERE

DETOURS INTO MAYHEM

PAUL CARTER

ALLEN&UNWIN

SYDNEY • MELBOURNE • AUCKLAND • LONDON

First published in 2013

Allen & Unwin
83 Alexander Street
Crows Nest NSW 2065
Australia
Phone: (61 2) 8425 0100
Email: info@allenandunwin.com
Web: www.allenandunwin.com

Cataloguing-in-Publication details are available from the
National Library of Australia
www.trove.nla.gov.au

ISBN 978 1 74331 276 6

Text design by Design By Committee
Typeset by Midland Typesetters, Australia
Printed in Australia by Pegasus Media & Logistics

10 9 8 7 6 5

For Sid

CONTENTS

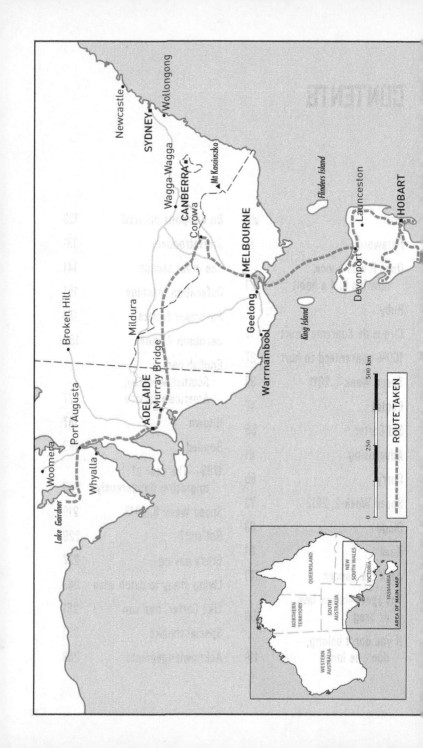

FOREWORD

THIS IS NOT a motorcycle, travel or adventure book—
it's just what constitutes my life and ranting about it in
book form again. I have no idea why people keep buying
them. If you have indeed done that then I thank you. Its
clinical name is 'Attempted observational humour based
on an obsessive-compulsive middle-aged man's attempt
to deal with various forms of self-induced task satura-
tion'. Life is sometimes all about managing expectations.
Bearing that in mind, I urge you to read on.

ONCE IT WAS A VICE. NOW IT'S JUST A HABIT

PICTURE THIS—a man with everything a man could hope for, the essentials in place, his personal pursuit of happiness completed. Solidified in a look, one that draws down deep, charging through his mind in resolute fulfilment. Just a brief look, a glance, nothing more, the clearest twinkle in a diamond eye from a wife that makes him all that he is and more.

Perfect to me, she is constantly surprising, unable to be ordinary, even when she tries, she doesn't care what other people are doing, or what they think or how much they have. She has style and grace, the ability to see beyond what's presented; she was born that way and it never fails to get my immediate and full attention.

That should do it, right? I can stop, just stop and smell the roses, and let the oil turn to stone in my motorcycles.

But it's not enough. Just to get to this point was considered impossible for so long—now it's here, what's next? It's not just death and taxes; it's not just growing older or watching your life speed-ramping into retirement. I need more, I need to challenge myself, otherwise I'm going to fail at middle-age bliss.

So I ask my wife, 'Can I go?' and she smiles and says, 'Sure, don't kill yourself.'

I carefully laid out my plan, my next bike challenge. Last time we did longevity and explored the distance end of bio-diesel; this time it's all about speed.

Two years ago in 2009 I was sitting in a bar in Adelaide opposite Dr Colin Kestell, the man behind the only properly compliance-plated, road-registered and insurable bio-diesel motorcycle in Australia. He had just agreed to let me take his bike on a trip right around the continent. He told me about another bike he was planning, one to break the motorcycle land-speed record in the alternative-fuel class—the record to beat was 210.203 kph. But there was no rider. It was right at that moment, while I sat there saying 'I want to do it' and he was eyeballing me through the bottom of his whiskey tumbler, that our friendship started.

We completed the ride around our great country on

the bio-diesel bike and now this new project, conceived back then, had come full circle as well. The land-speed bike was almost finished.

For the two years I made regular trips to Adelaide to talk through our plan, I watched the bike take shape slowly. At first it was literally just an engine sitting on a table, then the rear swing arm, and with each trip another component was built and added to the jigsaw. I watched, feeling a growing sense of purpose placate my need for adventure, adventure that wouldn't pull me too far from home, because home was getting busy. My wife, Clare, was pregnant while Lola, our three-year-old daughter, ran a total muck through our previously clean and calm home.

Another cusp approached in the form of a change in direction in my work as well. I decided to buy into a new-start business, along with five other oilfield mates.

The plan was simple, perfect; my lawyer and account-ant looked over the plan and basically said they wanted to buy into it, too. Good enough then, I thought.

'You read a book from beginning to end. You run a business the opposite way. You start with the end, and then you do everything you must to reach it.' These were the wise words of Harold Geneen, a successful American businessman most famous for heading up the ITT Corporation.

Going from an employee to an employer is a weird and worrying transition. My complete lack of skill sets to be a business owner also had me worried, but in the true and tried tradition of overspending we hired the right people to do it for us and thereby could go forth into the oil and gas market that at the time was wide open to a newcomer who could fill in the blanks that were severely lacking. My partners and fellow shareholders had been playing the corporate oil game for decades and we quickly grew with landed contracts and a growing client base.

I was suddenly in a place where I was making decisions, important ones that would affect the future of our business and its employees, and I loved it. I found myself in meetings that had follow-up meetings that ended up with some poor sod poring over pre-qualification tender documents as thick as the phonebook, while the meetings being held in the city would all end up in a middle-aged men's bar with more polished wood than a whorehouse. There we would sit and plot our business on large worn leather chesterfields, our neckties jutting out across unexercised bellies. Fine single malt was poured on company credit cards from decanters that took two hands to lift and looked like giant perfume bottles for men. I kept thinking it was all just a house of cards.

But I was wrong. Our ongoing success came down to one thing—people—hiring the right ones and knowing who to do business with. I couldn't believe how fast we grew, how efficient our financial team was. Within the first six months we had eighteen employees, our ISO certification and several other oil and gas specific certifications. Our ISO was the first to be granted in

Australia specifically for OCTG (oil country tubular goods) inspection, a strange industry way of referring to drill pipe, or any pipe for that matter, that's used in oil and gas. Our company performs non-destructive testing and inspection of basically everything that goes 'down hole', as well as all the kit used to lift and handle equipment on a drilling rig. So as well as ISO we had to get our NATA (National Association of Testing Authorities) accreditation as well, to deal with lifting inspection. We were audited almost every week by someone. Don't think for a second I'm suggesting it was easy, it wasn't. We just got lucky and after some teething we eventually had exactly the right team to make it work.

The learning curve was as fast and hard as my first desk job after leaving the rigs in 2007. So, as before, I checked my fragile male ego at the door and opened my ears, eyes and mind to new things.

RUBY

I CAME HOME one summer afternoon to a wedding invitation; my old friend Ruby was getting married in Sydney. In my past Ruby was a leading influence on all the drunkest, silliest and often flat-out dangerous things I've been involved with. You know, the things you do when you're young and on a crew change from a drilling rig with a house brick of US greenbacks burning a hole through your common sense. For a long time now Ruby had existed only in my memory, frozen the way I remember her, but like me she has grown up and I suppose you could say that, at least physically, we are proper adults now. This was going to be fun because it was Ruby's wedding. It would also be fun because, being Ruby's wedding, there was limitless piss-taking to do.

So Clare and I booked our tickets for the big day. Having lived in Perth for the past four years we took every opportunity to get back to Sydney.

Ah ... Sydney in the middle of summer. There's nothing quite like it. Our flight arrived on time and soon Clare, Lola and I arrived at the Randwick flat where Clare's sister Carrie lives. The next day Clare squeezed her three-month pregnant belly into a dress and we made for Bondi, leaving Lola with Carrie and a Wiggles DVD.

Ruby's wedding ceremony was faultless. It was good to see her so happy. Her husband, Rodrigo, is a gentle soul, full of pride and South American machismo balanced with humour and love. They're a seamless couple; they're even the same height.

Everyone was there from the old days, faces I had not pinged in years, all laughing, all having fun. The reception was in a renovated hall directly above the surf club, right on the beach. With the wonderful location and amazing view, Clare and I were both homesick for Sydney by the time dinner was served. We could see our old flat from where we now sat, those heady, child-free days now a distant memory buried under dirty nappies and morning sickness.

Dessert was closely followed by a bar fight, a drug bust, and my wife pulling me out of a photo booth the bride and groom had set up downstairs for the guests to play with. Clare ripped open the curtain, pulled the cigar out of my mouth and dragged me out with a curt 'Time to go' as more police ran upstairs.

Five a.m. found me sitting on the toilet in Carrie's flat, in denial. I thought back to the prawn entree, the unmistakable and all-too-familiar horror of what was about to ensue almost made me cry. Take my word for it, twenty years of working in the Third World and more than one case of dysentery leaves your body's ability to fight parasites strong but your mind scarred. If I was about to get sick, really sick, then those prawns must have been laced with nuclear waste.

I reckon they probably were, because both ends went nonstop for the next hour.

At 6 a.m. my phone beeped. It was Ruby texting me a question: 'Are you okay? Some people are a bit sick.'

Poor Ruby. Just what she didn't need. I had visions of how her big day turned out, somewhat ruined by the entire contents of a full jug of beer being flung by one man at another man but hitting Ruby square in the face. Sensitive to the situation, I replied, 'No, I'm losing my arse, I think a kidney just fell out.'

Then Clare's face appeared at the door, and the moment I saw her my heart jumped a beat.

'Get me to the hospital,' she said as she fell backwards into the hall. I don't know if it was just sheer will, but I managed to stop expelling prawns and staggered into the hall calling out to Carrie, then remembered she had just left to go to work. It's these moments, unplanned and frantic, where you find yourself. I pick up my wife, get her dressed, wake up my daughter and drag them out to our hire car. Clare lay there crying, a towel wrapped around her waist, another shoved down the back of my pants. 'Not again,' she wept, 'I can't lose another one.' Blood was soaking through the towel, and I drove hyperaware and terrified while Lola screamed in fear in the back seat. The hospital was, fortunately, only five minutes from the flat. I pulled up level at the doors, left the car running and ran in, holding my wife, her legs trailing blood on the white floor. Within seconds she was on a gurney and rushed down the corridor towards the emergency ward.

I stooped to pick up my daughter, scared and struggling to keep up. 'Just wait here, Mr Carter,' someone said as a firm hand was raised in my face and the emergency doors swung shut.

Lola looked up at me, confused and frightened, her face covered in tears, as I then fled towards the bathroom at the end of the corridor. I had to get my arse on a toilet seat.

'Are you doing a ka ka, Daddy?' she asked as I hurried into a cubicle.

'Daddy's not feeling very well, angel.' I was so grateful that she amused herself on tiptoe with the hand-dryer while I tried to compose myself.

We found a corner of the waiting room between a wall and a vending machine and sat on the floor. Wrapped in my jacket Lola eventually fell asleep. A long hour went by. The room bright in fluorescent light was quiet; there were only two other people there, reading old magazines. We all looked up as a doctor walked around the corner, his eyes scanning the room.

'Mr Carter,' he said, and hurried over to me. I stood up, leaving Lola asleep on the floor. 'Your wife is stable and sedated, but I'm afraid she's going to lose the baby.'

There was nothing I could say.

'You can come and see her now,' the doctor prompted. I picked up Lola and followed him down the hall.

Clare lay on a bed in hospital greens, full of morphine and anger. Morphine can make a sounding board for emotions that's big enough to raise the roof. 'This is fucked,' Clare said, as her head rolled from side to side. I put the still-sleeping Lola on a couch in the corner of the room and tried to comfort my wife, but she was livid with rage. I can't remember how much time went by. No one told me anything so I assumed the baby had been taken out and was already long gone. The doctor did say they had administered the maximum amount of morphine and that Clare should be much more sedated than she was. This is the fight that lives in my wife; she was not letting go, not for any reason.

Suddenly she sat bolt upright. 'Bathroom.' Her right hand ripped out the drip and amazingly she got to her feet in a second. I rushed in to steady her and help her to the toilet. As soon as she sat down she passed out, slumping forward into my shoulder. At that same moment our child fell out of her, into my left hand.

Time stopped, warm blood dripped between my fingers. Clare's unconscious weight started a lifeless roll to the left. I grabbed at her neck and sat her upright, reached across her shoulder and punched the big red

panic button on the wall. I could hear myself screaming inside that the first person through the door would
not be my daughter. But when Clare pulled the drip and
other wires off her body, an alarm must have gone off
somewhere, because two nurses burst through the toilet
door as soon as I hit that button.

The rest was another blur. Again my wife was rushed
away and another doctor was stopping me from following. I turned to look over my shoulder in time to see
a nurse leave our room with a blue cloth in her hands.
'Stop!' I yelled without thinking. I looked back at the
doctor, he was frozen, the nurse was static, halfway out of
the room, her eyes darting between the doctor and me.

Maintaining eye contact with the nurse, I walked across
the room that was now thick with a palpable awkward-
ness. My hands black with Clare's blood, I lifted the blue
cloth and there was our baby, in a stainless steel kidney-
shaped dish. Tears rolled off my nose onto tiny remains.
The floor dropped out from under me, while my heart
sank so low in my chest you could hear it breaking.

I raced over to Lola—somehow still wrapped in my
jacket and asleep on the couch in the corner—and swept
her up into my arms. 'You'll take me to Clare, right now,'
I said to the doctor. The doctor nodded his head and
held the door open for me.

Sometimes, if I have a fever or a nightmare, I see that
dish, in technicolour; it wakes me up every time.

Clare was being prepared for surgery and would not
be back in the conscious world for hours. I watched

numbly through a glass window for a while, aware only of my wife lying there even though the surgical team worked around her. Then Lola stirred and brought me back to earth and I walked away to the waiting room. I found myself back in the corner on the floor next to the vending machine, Lola now wide awake and bored out of her mind. But we didn't stay there for long.

'What's wrong, Daddy?' She bounced along next to me as my bowel decided it was time for round two.

Several hurried, sweaty trips to the toilet later I was exhausted, cried out and beaten. Then the vomiting started again. Eventually not bothering to get up and run to the toilet I just put my head into the rubbish bin next to the vending machine while Lola pointed out the fact that there was a distinct yellow hue going on.

'Does it hurt, Daddy?' I looked up over the bin at her big blue eyes. Slowly, the blurry background came into focus and I could see that the waiting room was now starting to fill with people, who glared at me in horror and disgust over copies of *Woman's Day*. The door opposite me flew open, surprising us as it had remained closed for hours.

'Are you okay? Have you been seen to?' A doctor in green get-up froze as soon as he saw us. I explained as much as I could about the last few hours and he quickly gathered us up and took us into his office. 'That's my toilet, you camp in there while I get you some medica-tion,' he said as he steered me towards a door then sat Lola down with some toys and books. A few minutes later the doctor returned with drugs to bung me up and hydrates to replenish my bone-dry system. But most importantly he told me he would check on Clare's situation.

I distracted myself over the next few hours by looking after Lola, cleaning the blood off my shirt, and pacing. I didn't allow myself to think about what I'd experienced, didn't let myself remember what I'd seen. All I wanted was my wife back, and fortunately for me it wasn't too long before we were together again.

Clare needed to stay in hospital after surgery, but typically she soon announced that she was ready to go home, even though she was still weak, woozy and couldn't walk. We left the hospital with Clare slumped in a wheelchair, her head buried in her hands, Lola crying because Mummy was upset, and me, pale, sweaty and splattered in bodily fluids—unrecognisable from the happy, healthy family who stepped off the plane yesterday. The sense of loss hanging around us leached in and out of every pore like an oil slick and threatened to squeeze the life out of everything.

As I pushed Clare out to the car park and our blood-stained hire car, an early model Ford transit van skidded to a stop directly in front of us. The van's sliding door flew open and five men in medieval chain mail and armour frantically spilled out onto the concrete. Their full metal outfits clattered together as they rushed around, barking orders at each other, then they dragged one knight who appeared to have a broadsword buried in his shoulder to the hospital doors.

Frozen by a curious blend of wonderment and horror, Clare and I silently watched their maniacal high-speed entrance. The van sat there in front us, its engine still running, several shiny helmets on its floor clinking together as the engine ticked over.

'Fuck,' said Clare. 'I thought I was having a bad day.'

CIRQUE DE SUPREME COURT

AT FIRST I sat there in the Supreme Court waiting to be tortured, while staring at the back of our opponent's head and imagining it exploding. Exploding while the QCs talk to each other and the judge shuffles his papers and listens to the litigation.

We had a good business plan, so good you could nail it to Donald and fling it over Trump Tower. But not according to the man whose head was about to explode, the 'plaintiff'. I'd just like to point out here that 'plaintiff' comes from the Anglo-French (the language spoken by descendants of the Norman invaders) for 'one who complains'.

We had apparently broken the first rule of business: 'Don't get sued.'

And the second rule of business: 'Don't go into business with anyone you don't know 100 per cent.' By that I mean performing due diligence that borders on stalking, crawling up their butthole with a microscope, getting charged with invasion of privacy and, when you're completely satisfied, hire a professional to do it all again.

The first two court sessions were interesting, but after two years I started to get really bored. The court case just turned into a normal part of our business operations, we budgeted for it, the months rolled by, and the bills rolled in. None of us went to court after the first few sessions unless we had to; we just let the legal teams do their thing and then report back afterwards. For a while I was convinced they all just closed the door and played tiddly-winks for an hour, ordered in lunch and drafted up the bills.

In fact, there were repetitious painstaking hour-long arguments, punctuated by eureka moments. There was passion, rivalry, hate and a healthy sprinkle of sheer blind chance. There were endless affidavits, subpoenas and what can only be described as embarrassing stalling tactics straight from the 'my dog ate my homework' school of law.

The partners stayed strong throughout all this bullshit. They'd been around long enough not to get rattled by the legal games and the psychological warfare that goes on, the attempts at intimidation that only really reflect fear and disappointment around the arena.

I soon learnt some tricks to deal with it, thanks to our director, Jason Theo, who had been through this kind of thing in business before. There are only a few people that I'll seriously listen to, whose advice I will take, and Jason is one of them.

The first trick was that if you can keep your wits about you, if you are lucky enough to lift the veil and see people for who they are, as opposed to the image they try so hard to project, you can become something far more imposing and real than an angry businessman—you have the clarity of mind to step back and breathe.

'After all,' said Jason, 'it's just money; it's just a pissing contest.' He was able to predict what was going to happen next in the legal saga, and I found the logic behind his thought processes very interesting: action and reaction based entirely on finances and ego.

So I found a weird peace in the middle of the maelstrom. For me, it was not personal at all, but to our opponents it was. Angry chests got inflated, stressed heart rates and voices were raised—they were in the bad kind of headspace that disrupts your life and leaves a scar on your soul. It was truly bizarre to watch.

During one particularly expensive session in court, Jason and I sat there while our opponents glared daggers at us and passed notes between themselves, occasionally leaning over to whisper something important directly into each other's ears, then look deeply onto their crotches, ponder for a moment, before looking up to glare at us again.

So Jason and I glared back, then I passed him my large imposing black diary in which I'd been studiously scribbling all morning. While he gave his best steely eyes across the room, I leaned over his shoulder and whispered into his ear, 'I drew a robot.'

Jason gave a slight nod, glanced down, poker face like solid marble, then his eyes flicked up again and fixed their cold stare on our antagonists while he passed the diary back. 'Nice robot,' he whispered.

Overall I'm actually grateful for the experience of having my back stabbed, balls kicked and being fisted with one big legal bill after another. In more than two years of litigation, reading threatening legal letters and paying attention to wise heads like Jason, I learnt volumes about keeping your business growing, your staff properly trained, happy and motivated, while you're freaking out, winning tenders, passing audits and certification requirements, and dealing with QCs and lawyers. I also learnt which pants chafe under my lodge apron following a three-course dinner, who I can trust in business and why men over 40 buy sports cars then drop dead.

Meanwhile, back on the home front, we were learning some lessons, too. Our all-knowing, all-expensive and all-consuming city council chose to relocate two large and entirely unemployed families into two state housing commission properties in our suburb. You can probably guess what happened next. Yep, within the first six weeks of our new neighbours moving in every house on our street had been broken into. Mine included.

The frightening thing was that the break-ins were happening between two and four in the morning while everyone was at home, asleep and vulnerable. The night we got done I'd crawled out of bed to get some water and was plodding down the hall into the kitchen and there was a man lifting the window off its frame. He looked like a ninja, completely dressed in black, while I looked almost pale blue and translucent, being bald, sun-deprived and completely naked. We shared a wide-eyed silent frozen moment, then he ran and I chased, as we fell into our respective roles like a couple of arche-typal cartoon characters. Only more absurd. Pick-axe handle in hand, my man bits wildly flapping about in the night air, I nearly left them on the fence before realising it was all a bit pointless and walked home naked for a cup of tea.

A week later and 25 grand less in the bank, our home can be locked down like a maximum security prison. Sure, it's overkill (as Clare likes to point out), but what are you going to do when the law is so ambig-uous about these things? I reckon that on confronting an intruder in his house, most red-blooded Aussie men will do whatever is necessary to defend his wife, young ones and all that he has worked so hard for. If I had to beat a man to death, then so be it. But in an effort to not let that scenario unfold, in our home there are now two different alarm systems and locks, impenetrably solid doors, security mesh, roller-shutters and enough motion-activated spotlights that if some muppet jumps over my fence at night again my yard will be visible from space.

Another side effect of our new neighbours was the redecoration of the bus stops. Every weekend, like clockwork, the bus stop on our street turned into an art gallery with wonderful modern tags and improvised street art bearing innovative titles like 'FUK U' or 'NIGGAS ON DUST' or the always popular and somewhat timeless 'CUNT'. Then every Monday morning the council truck would dutifully paint over all of the artwork, returning the bus stop to its original mental-hospital-wall vomit-green. This repetitious waste of paint went on for six months.

After everyone in the suburb had been thoroughly done over, every house, shed and car, every mailbox kicked, every bus stop vandalised, the council moved the families on to a new area to pick over. It's only a matter of time before they land in your neighbourhood, so remember, if you're running around naked with a pick-axe handle chasing intruders, the only winners will be the lawyers.

After our first year of operations, I went into another business venture. This time it started without breaking the first rule of business and grew at an equal rate without the legal bills. But this began to cut into my time and I was now juggling two businesses. I was doing it happily, though, because I had to make regular trips to talk to clients in Adelaide and this allowed me to spend time with Colin at the University of Adelaide where we would work on the bike.

She was growing into a monster.

I joined the Dry Lakes Racers Association (DLRA), the organisation that runs an annual event in Australia called 'Speed Week'. Speed Week began in 1985 and since its inception it has become a mecca for the rebellious petrolhead. For just one week a year, a few hundred mildly insane DLRA members gather, migrating like bogan salmon to a dry salt lake in the middle of nowhere (actually Lake Gairdner in South Australia). They will climb into or onto their machines—whether that's driving, riding or simply strapping themselves to a homemade rocket—and shatter the outback silence in a hell-bent effort to set new land-speed records and drink more piss. Some push the 400 kph mark; others get smashed and listen to Barnsey instead. In recent years a new class of competitor has surfaced—the non-fossil-fuel-burning type—so now, as well racers tear-arsing down the salt on machines with electric engines, there are those like myself on environmentally happier diesel.

But despite all my gibberish about congregating bogans and rockets, the DLRA is in fact a serious organisation. Every facet of Speed Week is very carefully planned and this means that as a member and competitor I need to know the rules. While we were building the bike we had the DLRA rulebook open all the time. The book itself is, however, thick and confusing. What class do I race in? How do I define a motorcycle that has a car engine in it? You know the sort of thing. Luckily, though, the DLRA scrutineers who pre-approve your machine and make sure it's safe and capable of doing what you want it to do were really helpful and eager to assist. I was immensely impressed with their level of care and skill, not to mention their pure enthusiasm.

Before too long I received the 'Operational Plan' from the DLRA, a detailed event schedule for Speed Week. Excitement reverberated around the university; even the mechanical engineering students who had helped design and build the bike, but who had now graduated and were out in the world, booked themselves in to be there so they could see her run down the track. All in all I was feeling really confident; everything had gone like clockwork over the last two years, the build, the planning, the paperwork, you name it. I even got booked to be the keynote speaker at the Association of Australasian Diesel Specialists (AADS) annual conference in Adelaide the day after we were slated to attempt the record.

Meanwhile, another plan had been ticking away in the background, as if I could put any more on my plate. Straight after Speed Week I was flying to Tokyo where I would jump on a Ural motorcycle with a sidecar, pick up my passenger and riding buddy Jocko, then ride around all four of Japan's islands. The fun part being that Jocko is a slightly disturbed adult male chimp with a passion for motorcycles and flower arranging. No, I'm not making this up.

I had been chipping away at this project for sixteen months; Jocko's owner, after I'd made several trips over there, agreed to let me explore the Japanese countryside with his pet. I got official permission to do it from the Japanese equivalent of our Roads and Traffic Authority and, as a result of that, also managed to find a fully qualified primate veterinarian who's into motorcycles willing to come along in case Jocko twisted off one day and tried to eat someone and needed to be tranquillised. I had the bike customised to accommodate Jocko with a cleverly designed harness and he even had his own riding gear including helmet and goggles. Bike builder and close mate Matt Bromley was at the time finalising his build of all the bikes for the upcoming but severely delayed filming of *Mad Max Fury Road*. Matty gave the bike the once-over for me and finetuned the sidecar for Jocko's hairy arse. As usual, he did an amazing job.

I spent many years in my past working in Japan on drilling rigs and made some lifelong friends there. Most of them live between Nagaoka and Niigata on the west coast of Japan's main island of Honshu. They helped with the importation and registration of the bike, and organised a storage facility to house it and all the spares. Their contacts in oil and gas meant this happened very smoothly through the port of Chiba, then the bike was road-freighted up to storage in the port of Sendai, where it sat poised like a coiled spring in a small tin shed near the mouth of the Natori River.

So all the prep work for that project was also done, and it was ready and waiting for me to arrive, fuel up the bike and go.

Between business trips to Brisbane and Adelaide, between meetings and the Supreme Court, between Lola's Saturday morning swimming lessons (with me standing in a languid pool surrounded by ten screaming smelly brats producing a minimum 60 per cent urine content) and mowing the lawn on Sundays, I found myself thinking about the salt lake, the speed and eventually Japan's clean, safe roads beckoning from across the globe. I pictured Jocko and me enjoying a cold beer at the end of the first day's riding, parked with the wonderful snow-capped Mt Kurodake in the background while the vet looked on and polished his dart gun.

Happy days.

100% GUARANTEED TO HURT

BUT IT WAS not to be.

Of all the things that could have stopped my bike tour around Japan with a chimpanzee, I would never have thought of a tsunami.

On 11 March 2011 Japan suffered its worst disaster; the wave that hit Sendai was 40 metres high, it swept inland for 10 kilometres wiping out everything that couldn't get out of its way. Including Jocko. Meanwhile I stood in my lounge room dumbfounded in front of the evening news with the phone in my hand and no one answering.

Of course, I hadn't insured the bike or any of the bike gear. I thought it was safe and secure; if anyone should understand what Mother Nature can do with the ocean, it's me. My learning curve continues.

I started to make arrangements to go to Japan to salvage what I could. 'No, stay there,' said my friend Taka. 'There's nothing left to look for.' He added that a nuclear power plant in the area had some big problems, too.

So there I was with two businesses running my arse ragged, severe sleep deprivation, a Supreme Court trial looming, a land-speed world record attempt campaign to organise, and now Jocko was dead and my Matt Bromley bike and sidecar gone . . . what else could happen? I sat in my office at the end of the day pondering this when my phone rang.

'I'm pregnant,' said my wife.

I jumped out of my seat and punched the air. 'AWESOME, BABY!' She was laughing. 'I'm on my way home.' I was suddenly full of pure joy and, grabbing my jacket from behind my chair, I paused to shut down my computer, and that's when it happened.

My body decided to scare the bejesus out of me and pulled a stunt that had me splayed on the floor under my office desk in massively violent spasms of pain. I was convinced in those first few minutes that my appendix had just exploded or that I was having an aneurysm.

'Right, so, that's it then,' the voice of reason crackled over the PA system in my head.

I vomited across the carpet, fighting to catch my breath as the pain hit in hard, overwhelming waves, while clinging desperately to the vinyl armrest of my desk chair. I was being tazered by my brain.

'This is how you end,' the PA announced, 'alone under your desk in an empty office building.' I'd always pictured something much more sedate or violently fast, but that's life, isn't it?

The pain suddenly backed off, enough for me to unclench my fists. My right hand hurt so I rolled over onto my back and lifted my arm into view. I had been holding the chair so tightly that my fingernails had bent back on themselves and my fingers were bleeding. Moaning and scrambling I managed to drag myself to my knees and phone for an ambulance before the next wave of pain knocked me back into a puddle on the floor.

Dr Brooks had a kind face, spoke with his hands and was very reassuring as I arrived at the emergency department of the hospital. There was no stuffing around, though. 'You're going straight in to have an MRI, Paul,' he said. As the giant machine wound up and slowly began the search for my brain, I thought about John Lennon, not my wife or kid as I was supposed to, and by the time I came back out I'd moved on to the complete works of Paul Weller.

'Kidney stone,' said the smiling Dr Brooks. 'Extremely painful. The nearest thing a man can experience to child-birth.' Great, I'll try to remember that, I thought.

Twenty years of standing on the drill floor in the tropics while being dehydrated. 'I'm fuckin' paying for it now,' I said loudly as I leant against the wall in the emergency department toilet, fumbling at my hospital robes with fingers wrapped in Elastoplast now holding my fingernails in place. I bit down hard as blood flowed into the urinal. The kidney stone was tearing everything up on its way out, it felt like I was trying to piss a brick with a tractor nailed to it. I let fly with enough bad language, blood and wall-punching to make the guy waiting outside fall over himself in an effort to get out of my way as I emerged, bloodstained and wild.

Morphine arrived in my arm like an old friend with a fifth of whiskey and a sad story. Soon a prickly heat rush rolled across my forehead and down my spine like a white-hot jungle centipede. 'Ohhh yeah, lower me down, you gorgeous hospital health professionals.' I smiled crookedly at the doctor. Tears streaked wet tracks across my crow's-feet and doglegged down my cheeks to pool in my jugular notch.

'Are you alright?' he checked my pulse.

'I'm fine.' I focused on not sustaining the grin and tried not to think about my brother-in-law Mathew; the drugs had made my brain revert to the last time I had this much morphine smashed into my body. Four years ago in Longreach Hospital, slap-bang in the middle of outback Queensland, with a toothless and obviously mentally disturbed pensioner in the bed next door, Matty's bent jokes about my poor neighbour and the nurses and my condition had made me laugh so hard I nearly choked to death. So all's well with morphine and me.

I was ushered into a treatment room where I lay on a bed in a corner, staring at a soundless TV suspended from the ceiling, trying to lip-read the conversation on the screen. Sudden and frenzied activity broke through my morphine heat haze and I could hear doors slamming and garbled conversation. Two paramedics circled the corner wheeling a patient who appeared to be a rather nasty-looking junkie. He had just been the lucky recipient of a free government heart start, but instead of saying 'thank you' and slipping into his clean hospital jammies for a cuppa and bickie, he was thoroughly pissed off about it, swearing and punching on. Moments after his wild punches connected with one of the paramedics, a cop appeared and slammed his elbow down on my noisy neighbour's chest, causing his screams to stop and mine to start. The nasty bastard had just lost his arse. At the same time as superfly on my left did his business, the elderly lady on my right, who had just arrived after falling and breaking a hip, did her business all over her curtained-off area.

'Unbelievable,' I said, then I started laughing. The more they screamed, the more I laughed. I knew it was wrong, but that just made it funnier. And the more people started looking at me, horrified and offended, the worse it got. I was laughing, crying, I got the hiccups, I nearly shat my own pants.

Dr Brooks appeared, all focused, serious and kind amid the screaming, shitting and laughing. He politely explained that they couldn't move me to a private room at the moment so could I please stop laughing. I held my breath, bit my lip, composed myself and asked for some headphones so I could watch the movie.

Nine hours later Ayers Rock, red and huge, finally exited my body. I went home to have a shower and drink 600 litres of water.

SPEED WEEK 1.
2011

ON ANY BIKE, in any language, 300 kph is a big number. But doing 300 kph on an untested experimental motorcycle could be considered a reliable way to kill yourself.

Our motorcycle, the BDM-SLS or Bio Diesel Motorcycle Salt Lake Special, is 4 metres long, weighs almost half a tonne, and runs on an experimental fuel called 'Clean Diesel' produced by Australian company Linc Energy. Linc pushed the experimental envelope to produce it, like we did with the bike, and produce it they did. I can't really describe the process to you in basic terms because I can't spell most of the words the Linc engineers use when they try to explain it to me, let alone understand what they mean. But so you have a rough idea of what Clean Diesel is, here goes.

The back story is a simple one. I was going to run the BDM-SLS on bio-diesel fuel derived from used cooking oil, just like I did with the bio-bike that I rode around Australia in my last book. Part of the reason I wrote that book was to make a point about the future of fuel, about our chronic dependency on it. Without fuel—I'm talking good old-fashioned petrol—we descend into anarchy faster than you think. We have played the oil game at a level that's hard to define in print globally, and at any human or environmental cost, every day since before the end of World War Two. You could pretty much say that WWII just morphed into a secret energy war that has raged on since. Now the fossil fuel system is just too big and powerful to stop, and many people think, what's the point?

For me, the dream of a viable alternative fuel, sustainable at the bowser, was the idea of diesel derived from garbage—turning used cooking oil to fuel. It's not a hard or expensive process, and our country goes through a massive amount of diesel every day; our country is run on the trucking industry alone. I never did the maths on it because I got despondent and utterly frustrated with the system. But, having said that, just think about how much oil your average fast-food burger joint chucks into landfill every year—there is an inexhaustible supply of the base product. All our public transport, trucking and industry could be fuelled on bio-diesel. We would suddenly produce 75 per cent less carbon emissions.

One of the first things that hit me when I was riding around Australia on used cooking oil was the amount of people in rural areas, or for that matter anywhere outside the cities, who instantly recognised that I was riding a bike that was powered by bio-diesel. That was because they all have little secret stills of their own. On average, every rural roadhouse would chuck out about 20 litres of used cooking oil a month. Instead, a local farmer will take it home to brew cheap fuel. It was like they suddenly identified me as a friend. But their praise and acknowledgement was hushed and whispered. Why so secretive? Because if our government were to find their bio-diesel stash it would slap a big fine on them. Instead of encouraging the potential of bio-diesel, the Australian government fines them and sits back to enjoy the fuel tax revenue system as it is, while at the same time imposing a carbon tax on everyone. It's a pointless bureaucratic joke that goes beyond just greed and propels it into stupidity.

Companies like Linc Energy have taken their ideas for cheap sustainable diesel to our government and were told to fuck off.

They said, 'But we have a great system that we can prove works, can we show you how it works?'

'No,' said our government. 'And if you contact us again, we will have you all tazered and made to perform unnatural sex acts to a 400-pound Queensland wild sow.'

Right, so you get the picture.

Despite the lack of government support, Linc just went ahead and did it anyway. It cost them hundreds of millions.

There are shallow coal formations all over the eastern states of Australia, and Linc drill into these formations and, in a nutshell, pump oxygen into the coal and set it on fire. Not in a 'burn the house down' way but more of a 'combustion that is occurring not burning' kind of way. Unlike mines that dig a giant fuck-off hole in the ground and gasify the coal on the surface, the UCG (underground coal gasification) synthesis gas that comes out of Linc's well is the source of the clean diesel— basically, they convert the syngas to liquid fuel. Linc built a demonstration facility near Chinchilla in Queensland to prove all this. This facility is the only one of its kind in the world; it has trial generators and a GTL (gas to liquid) pilot plant. Linc has successfully combined UCG and GTL technologies to produce high-quality hydro-carbon liquids from synthesis gas.

Like many great ideas and some really bad ones—such as intercontinental ballistic missiles, genetic mutation, cloning, supersonic flight, brain surgery on a conscious person, atomic weapons and killing lots of people because you don't like their banking habits, colour, religion, sexual orientation, political beliefs or they're just not German enough—the Nazis were the first to come up with this syngas process. German engineers produced diesel in a similar fashion when their supply lines got cut off in Russia. Some clever Nazi probably got a panzer running on seawater in 1941, but then immediately disappeared along with everyone they ever knew . . . ever.

As far as I'm concerned, Linc and their Clean Diesel is a happy viable middle ground that works. And thank god at least someone is doing something different, not the usual few million spent on a flash TV ad campaign about how much they care about the environment and the future with lots of shots of cute kids playing on a beach and getting hugged by their wonderfully good-looking happily married parents. Or full page ads in the newspaper showcasing a snappy tag-line like 'Human Energy' or 'Fuelling Good' which some advertising copywriter charged a small fortune for or an enhanced image of a happy functional nuclear family cavorting in a huge green field because they care . . . Fuck off. We know we need petrol, we need all of it, every hydrocarbon product ever made, but don't expect us to buy these cheesy ads, for fuck's sake, it's insulting. Just ask BP.

Drilling is drilling. It's dangerous. It's a hole in the ground. Mother Nature can turn around and shit all over it if she wants to, or there's just some other freak accident, or good ol' human error, or greed, or a combination of the lot. I say, by all means, drill—of course I'm going to say that—but break it and you pay for it.

Here's where the man behind the company that will set the pace for fuel supply in Australia enters the story, quietly and with no fanfare. Linc Energy's Peter Bond walks into a meeting I'm sitting in. He's a big man, six foot, broad shoulders, in jeans and a casual shirt; he fixes me with a strong blue gaze and shakes my hand. At the time I have no idea I'm meeting our country's foremost fuel entrepreneur. Needless to say, Peter is completely affable, warm and not at all the corporate giant I had pictured. Within moments I understand that he is all about transparency, accountability, and sustaining the environment he's drilling in. In fact, all the things I've spent twenty years waiting to see oil and gas companies not just say but actually do. It's like slipping into a warm bath. I'm hearing the future of affordable, sustainable fuel in our country being mapped out across the conference table. I'm in drilling nirvana; I have to force myself not to clap when he finishes speaking.

So I had my fuel, I had my bike, I needed to test it. Speed Week was less than a month away.

Over the past two years, Associate Professor Colin Kestell, the University of Adelaide and I had put a lot of effort into this event. Our objectives were straight-forward:

- Select an engine, capable of enough speed but not too heavy.
- Test the engine air–fuel maximums.
- Develop the power train to integrate the engine with the chassis.
- Design and build the chassis.

- Design the frame and fairing including full CFD (computational fluid dynamics) analysis in 3D.
- Test a scale model in a wind tunnel to verify CFD results.
- Select the right gearbox.
- Link the gearbox to the engine.
- Combine the engine, gearbox, transmission, front triple clamp and fork geometry with rear swing arm within the frame and fairing.
- Fabricate rims and select tyres.
- Test electronic fuel management system and gauges, controls, linkages, seat and rider position analysis.
- Dyno test.
- Speed test.
- Break world record.
- Get drunk.

Dr Colin Kestell stood under the open rollerdoor looking into the expansive mechanical engineering workshop with a coffee in his hand and a slightly distracted expression on his face. It turned into a smile as I stopped by his shoulder and punched him on the arm.

Two years ago, Colin and I had collaborated, along with his students spanning several graduating years, to build 'Betty' the bio-bike and get all the way around Australia on bio-diesel made from used cooking oil. Betty was a pig—a shuddering, painful death pig. She tried to kill me, she tried to shove her left handlebar up my arse, she put me in Longreach Hospital for four days with cracked ribs and a damaged rotator cup, she made me beg, but I loved her. She was built on a shoe-string budget, a Frankenstein motorcycle running an 8-horsepower irrigation-pump engine that vibrated so violently I had residual nerve damage in my hands for three months after I completed the ride.

Betty spawned another bio-diesel monster, but this time there were no cute names, no making do, no irrigation-pump engines. This time we had a 1.7-litre, 90-kilowatt, 60-horsepower Holden Astra turbo diesel engine teamed with a five-speed Harley Davidson Dyna gearbox. The Bio Diesel Motorcycle Salt Lake Special was designed for one purpose only—to go fast on a salt lake in the middle of nowhere.

The BDM-SLS has a very wide frame, long wheel-base (more than 3 metres) and is made of steel. So it looks and sounds cumbersome and underpowered, but in fact this is what you need to get up to speed on the salt. Weight is essential to get the power down on the back wheel and avoid wheel spin, and it also aids stability on the salt, especially with crosswinds; the length will also help in these unique conditions.

No expense was spared—she was getting close to six figures. We had been working on this project for more than two years and this trip to Adelaide was the one I had been dreaming about for so long—the one where I get to ride her for the first time.

Just the thought of going to a place like Lake Gairdner had been exciting me, to fly across our great land, look down and see endless red and orange earth occasionally interspersed with sparkling white salt lakes. The lakes are so remote, so untouched. My nose pressed up against the perspex, I had been gazing at them on every flight to and from Brisbane for a long time, waiting for Speed Week to arrive, amazed at the beauty of the harsh inland. Our salt lake was 550 kilometres northwest of Adelaide, one of the most remote places in Australia.

With Speed Week starting on a Monday, I arrived on Saturday morning so we had the whole day to pack everything before leaving on Sunday for a week of intense salt-skimming balls-to-the-wall speed trials.

Saturday was mad. Colin had been in touch with the DLRA as there were concerns about the weather, the potential for rain being monitored diligently. I had mates arriving from Brisbane and Matt Bromley was also en route from Sydney, on a bike of course. The whole event pulsed a viable sense of purpose into everyone as we scurried about packing, re-packing, checking and double-checking everything twice. By lunchtime our gear was good to go, the bike was ready and sitting in her custom-made dual-axle trailer, two support vehicles were laden with fuel, bike spares, tools, tents, water, tarps, food, the list went on and on.

It was really exciting for me to have two of my close mates, Simon Hann and Howard Fletcher, joining me on this adventure. Both blokes have busy family lives and careers to juggle, being the good citizens they are these days. Of course, it wasn't always so. Both Simon and Howard were oilfield men in the traditional sense, and by that I mean they used to be bad, medievally bad. They used to have their names on their shirts, they had tattoos, rode motorcycles fast, drank to get drunk, never went to the doctor and had a keen interest in self-destruction.

But that was the past. They had turned the successful corner, bent their ways and embraced the new environmentally friendly all-you-can-eat oilfield salad bar system, and now they are good. So good, in fact, that they are husbands and fathers, they exercise, watch their diet, have regular health checks, don't smoke and only have the occasional drink. They got educated; they have lots of qualifications now and sometimes wear ties to work. Simon looks like he never battered a muppet in a bar fight. Howard looks like my accountant, except my accountant doesn't know how to make napalm and never ran through the jungle naked with a large piece of burning toilet paper protruding from his clenched butt cheeks.

When Simon and Howard got out of the cab at the workshop, you would not see the oil men inside for the clean veneer of corporate respectability glistening in the sun, their respective halos twinkling.

'You look like shit,' Howard says, grinning.

There were man-hugs all round before I shoved them into a university car and we drove across Adelaide to pick up two fully kitted four-wheel-drive campers. There is very little accommodation on Lake Gairdner (the Mt Ive homestead nearby has some cabins and rooms but they're just too far away from the action), so we opted for the motorhome option while on the salt.

Two hours later we all pulled up at the motel I'd booked in the middle of Adelaide's main strip and general drunk-ridden vomit-slicked Hindley Street for Saturday night. The plan was to head out to the salt lake on Sunday morning then stay in the campervans. However, Speed Week coincides with the annual Clipsal 500 V8 car races so every hotel, motel, shitty flea-bag dump decided to triple their rates and demand full payment in advance. I didn't realise that every available hotel room that was remotely decent had been booked months ago, so in my last-minute haste I only managed to get a shared room for three in an excuse for a motel.

'Right, so, Mr Carter, that's a room for three and parking for three vehicles for Saturday, 19 March.' The lady sounded very nice on the phone.

'Yes, all good,' I said.

'And in case you didn't see our website, sir, we are gay-friendly here.'

'Pardon?' I said.

'Our motel is very gay-friendly.'

'Well, ah, okay, that's good to know, but I'm not gay.'

'Of course, you're not, Mr Carter, I just thought I would mention that our motel is—'

I cut her off. 'Yes, I know, very gay-friendly.'

As we pulled up at the motel looking for the parking spaces I'd also paid for in advance, the horror started to set in. The directions basically had us parked in a real rapetastic overgrown lot off a seedy alleyway at the rear of what looked like a derelict building. I phoned to make sure we had the right place. Yep, this was our gay-friendly motel.

They'd slapped me with a $490 per night bill for a horrid little toilet of a room. Simon walked in and looked like I'd just crapped in his latte. 'Fuckin' hell, Pauli, this is the best you could do? I wouldn't let my dog kip in this dump—and they think we're gay.'

Howard set to work fixing the aircon unit that looked older than me. It groaned then sparked a bit before shuddering to life, shaking the room and making the whole experience feel like a railroad boxcar on the way to the annual gay festival in gay town.

We went out that night full of excitement and antici-pation. Colin was set to meet us for dinner, but he was running a bit late. While I was standing outside the bar next to the restaurant on Hindley Street enjoying the rabble of perpetual wallopingly drunk teenagers all on a full-blown binge-drinking exercise in liver demolition, he called me and as soon as I heard his tone I knew it was bad.

'I'm so sorry, mate, but Speed Week just got cancelled,' he said.

Colin explained that the DLRA officials had arrived at Lake Gairdner and discovered two things: it was rain-ing hard, and the entrance from the land to the salt was badly damaged. There's a special rubber ramp that you're supposed to use when you take your vehicle onto the salt, otherwise the salt gets damaged. It's simple, really—the ramp's right there, you just need to set it up and off you go. But there's always an exception, some selfish idiot. Just prior to the DLRA's arrival, a TV commercial was shot on the salt involving a four-wheel-drive cruising about on the salt and making pretty circles with its wheels, revealed at the end of the ad via a chopper shot—wow, how clever. They didn't bother to use the ramp, though, and fucked up the entrance. That severely upset the Indigenous community and the DLRA. Mother Nature then decided to turn Lake Gairdner back into a lake, raining heavily over the past two days. Even though the lake had been known to dry up rapidly, the DLRA made the call to cancel the event.

I was floored with disappointment. All the work, the planning, everything—this was our shot and it just got taken away.

Colin arrived at the pub soon after and we all sat down and stared at the floor. None of us it took it well. Colin was philosophical, of course, but I could tell he was crushed. The other Speed Week crews were equally subdued; it was like we'd gone from a buck's party to a wake.

'All that gear and the vehicles are non-refundable,' I moaned into my beer. I'd just spent eight grand for nothing. What now?

Well, we did what motivated, capable, intelligent, educated men do in these situations and got drunk.

At some point between beer and whiskey o'clock, Colin came up with a brilliant idea and suggested we depart for the test track in the morning and at least ride the bike. Then he jumped on the phone to wake someone up and organise it. Simon booked himself the first available flight back to Brisbane—I was sorry to see him go but he does have a whole drilling division of a major multinational to run, so he was packed and out of our shitty gay motel before we could convince him to have another Bloody Mary. Howard stayed on. 'I want to see it run, mate,' he said, grinning.

Speed Week may have been officially cancelled, but there's no stopping a bunch of lunatics with a fast bike and a test track.

EAGLES

SUNDAY MORNING, first light, grey impending clouds collided overhead rumbling a death rattle that hammered back the fact that Speed Week was cancelled. The dank mood that hung in the air mixed with our hungover beer breath as we quietly and painfully pulled out of Adelaide. The drive was silent—Colin, Howard, Ed and Steve, one of the mechanics from the uni, all sat deep in post-beer thought.

Two hours later we pulled off the highway into Tailem Bend test track, 100 kilometres southeast of Adelaide. A former Nissan facility, the test track was now privately owned. It had a 1.4-kilometre straight that I was about to point the bike down and hopefully she would give me the good news.

The rain kicked in closely followed by powerful gusts running left to right across the track. We all paused as if to silently ask, 'Should we stop and wait for the weather to change?' But we all knew it was only going to get worse.

The bike slowly rolled out the rear doors of its giant trailer and sat there in the rain on the tarmac, looking for a fight.

We set about prepping her for the first run. The rear fairing was removed, bolts checked and marked, chain checked and lubed, diesel poured into her small tank while I peeled on my body armour: a leather racing suit, boots, helmet and finally gloves.

My mouth went dry as I threw my leg over her massive bulk and settled into the seat. Her frame had been built around mine—it was like putting on a tailored smoking jacket in a gentleman's club for sociopaths. But I had no fear of consequences, none at all.

Steve strapped the red emergency stop cord to my wrist and flipped up the three bright red switch covers concealing the fuel pump start, fuel management module and the engine start button. He primed the throttle and flicked the first two switches and the bike whirred, the digital instrument cluster blinking to life, tiny bulbs glowing green and needles jumping to indicate fuel and oil pressure, battery levels, engine temp, oil temp, engine revs and speed. He looked directly at me, grabbing the sides of my helmet: 'Push it.'

I nodded, looked down over the metre-wide front end surrounded by a massive green fairing, inside a cockpit of lights, gauges and switches. Fear suddenly rose up into my throat. Before it reached my head I pushed the engine start button and she barked, shuddering alive with that unmistakeable diesel rumble.

'In your own time, mate,' Colin said. He was standing with Steve to my left. Straight ahead was 1.4 k's of grey wet track. At the other end was a series of orange traffic cones indicating where I needed to grab the brakes. We had been over the length of the track, removing any stones and looking for irregularities; I'd made a mental note of a small pothole about halfway down slightly right of centre.

Rain streaked down the windshield as I leant well forward into the bike's almost prone riding position. I pulled in the clutch and selected first gear; she jerked slightly as the gear dropped in with a reassuring thunk. I glanced down at my revs and gunned the throttle a couple of times, the needle rising and falling with the engine . . . It was time to hit the playground.

I tuned into the sound of her engine as my right hand rolled the throttle back and my left released the clutch. She pulled hard, rolling forward and gathering speed much faster than I'd expected. I slipped down and back into the seat base and let my feet find the pegs. Laying my chest down over the front end, I focused on the horizon and popped her into second. She was smooth and accelerating as fast as my regular bikes do.

Third gear at 2500 rpm and 100 kph dead straight no problems, I cruised to the end of the track and discovered she has the turning circle of a battleship. The wind gusts had been picking up and I was very conscious of them and the wet track, but the bike was just so big and heavy it reassured me, so by the time I'd gone down the track four times I was ready to see just how fast we could go.

Again I found third gear within six seconds, but this time I rolled the throttle wide open through the gearbox, red-lining the gear changes. She pulled away hard and I found my position behind the windshield, no wobbles, tank-slapping or body-tensing moments. She roared as her revs hit 3500, still pulling away in third. At 160 kph I popped her into fourth. There was a surge of power; at full throttle north of 4000 rpm she took off like the horizon just stole her handbag.

The blur of the trackside shrunk into the periphery as my vision fixed on the end of grey line ahead. The first orange traffic cone was coming up fast; I held the throttle open although everything told me not to, glanced down, passing 170 kph.

I don't know what the odds are, you tell me, on a windy, rainy day, but right at that moment, not one but two eagles decided to fly across the track at head height.

I pinged the movement in my line of sight, stopped my brain from making my reflexes roll off the throttle, and smashed on. At that speed hitting an eagle wasn't going to make any difference, it was all in the hands of the gods now.

Bird one didn't see me hammering at him but bird two did; he slammed on the brakes, looking for height, while I passed through the gap between them. The funny thing is, when I tell friends these sort of stories, as I've always done, they invariably say, 'Bullshit' then 'Did you get a photo?' Well, this time I did; one of the guys was snapping away and the moment was caught on camera.

After that nothing else existed except the howling engine. Vibrations suddenly shaking her under me, I broke my fixation on the end of the track to dart my eyes down—177 kph and still accelerating hard.

This sort of bike, at this speed, on a track in these conditions will, I can assure you, concentrate your mind in a way you can never replicate again. I had to slow down my brain; it wanted to process double the input at 170 than it did at 70.

Piercing the static air at this speed was harder for her than learning the Russian alphabet backwards. Pushing through it for me was not just a case of holding on at full throttle. Think about all those multimillion-dollar Formula One wind-tunnel-tested racing cars you occasionally see getting flipped over or hurled into a tree by the beast that is air resistance. Parts shear off, vibrate to bits, flat-out shatter or make so much noise you can feel it in your teeth. The bike suddenly started doing all these things.

As I passed the last orange traffic cone, where I was supposed to grab the brakes, I felt the gods of speed laugh and welcome a new convert to the fold. I pictured the bleached white salt stretching into the void until the boundary between the sky and the horizon is blurred . . . then the beast, its eyes dead and dark, leant over the fairing and punched me straight in the face.

The entire front end of the bike suddenly lifted effortlessly into the air, my horizon and the disappearing track replaced with sky. My heart and time stopped, every muscle went hypersensitive. I rolled off the power and the front wheel came down fast, hitting the track and staying straight, thank god. I, however, was not straight. While my front wheel was up in the air, the crosswind had pushed the front end a few inches to the right and I was now heading straight towards the edge of the track. The problem was that unlike a conventional motorcycle, I couldn't just lean over and correct my line because this bike was a metre wide and only a few inches off the ground; if I did lean to correct my direction I would have bottomed out the engine on the asphalt and game over. So I jumped on both brakes, squeezing harder as the edge of the track was now out of view and somewhere underneath us.

She stopped a few feet from the end of the track and a few inches from the edge.

My heart started up again.

I cranked my head around to see the boys racing towards me in the car. They screamed to a stop next to me and jumped out.

'Jesus, fuck, man, what happened?' Steve could hardly get his words out. 'You nearly took off.'

I was high as a kite. 'You tell me, mate, you built the fuckin' thing.'

For a few moments we all stood there in the rain, dumbfounded, just looking at the bike with a mixture of awe and fear.

Then Colin's rocket-scientist voice cut through the silence. 'Oh dear,' he said without looking up from his clipboard which he was busily scribbling on.

Turns out with all the wind-tunnel testing and design, everyone forgot to compensate the suspension and fairing angle for my weight. There is a metal plate under the engine, part of the rules for salt-lake racing because you can't drop any fluids on the track. So when I'm sitting on the bike, that flat and level plate is at a positive angle into the wind, and that means when we hit a certain speed, the bike lifts off.

Colin took some measurements and crunched the numbers right there on the track, muttering to himself like the mad scientist, and after a couple of minutes looked up from his clipboard. 'Yeah, 177 is enough to generate the lift required to pick up the bike.'

'No fuckin' shit,' I said from behind the car where a nervous pee was now being held onto while I tried to climb out of leathers and gloves before I had a real accident.

So, given that the bike nearly broke a world record for flight, albeit unintentionally—and I nearly copped an eagle in the head at 170 clicks—it's probably a good thing we missed Speed Week that year. It was back to the drawing board; we had work to do and a whole year to wait before our next crack. But that's okay, one thing I do have is lots of patience.

SID CARTER

MY SON, ACCORDING to the doctor, was not going to get out and into Wally World in the conventional fashion, he was just too big. So it was decided early in the pregnancy that Clare would need a caesarean section and before I knew it we were waiting sweaty-palmed and nervous in a veritable production line of very pregnant mothers. Lola was at home with Clare's mum—'The Cath'—who had flown over from Sydney just like she did for us when Lola was born. I was hugely grateful to her; I simply couldn't face the thought of having Lola in another hospital with me and time to kill while Clare was going through hell in some room I wasn't allowed into. At least this time I wasn't projectile vomiting and no one appeared to have a broadsword buried in their chest.

One by one the ladies went through the big double doors with their men walking alongside. The men all had that expression on their face—faking the confident supportive role, but inside we're thinking, 'Thank fuck I don't have to do this shit.' It's closely related to the facial expression we pull when we have to stop and ask for directions or if we're at fault in a car accident.

Clare was going in next, we were cool, I was fetching her magazines, she was totally calm, I thought I was actually doing a pretty good job of distracting her mind from the guy in the green mask next door who was going to carve her up like a Sunday roast.

Then the call came in. 'Mrs Carter, we're ready for you.'

The room was as I remembered when Lola was born, the giant metal arm coming out of the ceiling holding three round flashlights bent at the elbow like a transformer just put its arm in the wrong place while rummaging through the attic. The table-tennis set-up under the arm with the sheet strung up across the middle so Clare couldn't see the Green Hornet split her open like a watermelon and dive both hands in up to the elbow. Busy people scooted about in white wellies and hairnets, I found my stool next to the table and faked a positive reassuring smile; small talk seemed so pointless, my mind went blank. She must be shit-scared by now.

The joyful masked anaesthetist leant in and started talking to us, but I was suddenly not listening as there was an immediate and very painful sensation growing in my flank; I even turned to look because it felt like someone had just tripped over and buried a scalpel in my back. Clare was already masked up, the Green Hornet was carving, my pain was wild but I blanked it out in time for Sid to appear at the top of the curtain, shrivelled and purple. Clare was happy but couldn't see that from where I was standing she looked like a magician's accident.

Sid was a 9-pound whopper. I was a little shocked at the size of his member and pointed.

'Oh, that's perfectly normal,' said a masked lady, handing me the scissors so I could cut through Sid's umbilical cord.

'Normal,' I mused. It looked like a can of guinness with a cow's heart on the end. My boy was a miracle.

There was just enough time to kiss my wife before she was whisked off to have the lower half of her body re-attached. Sid was also whisked off to have his nob recorded in the *Guinness World Records*. I smiled reassuringly as mother and child left then collapsed on the floor; I recognised this pain. After some writhing and moaning, I thought I saw the Green Hornet hovering over me, bloodied and wielding a knife, then the rest was a familiar blur.

'Kidney stone,' smiled Dr Brooks.

'Yes, I know, it's just like childbirth,' I moaned.

The doctor nodded, smiled kindly and calmly explained that I was about to pass another boulder, this time from the other kidney. Then he gave me morphine and out came what I was thinking: 'My wife's upstairs having just produced a giant penis with a small baby attached to it. The Green Hornet's up there sewing her together again right now.'

'I beg your pardon?' Dr Brooks said as he checked my pulse.

I was wheeled into a room, a quiet, dark, private, junkie- and poo-free room. I think I called The Cath but it was foggy; I vaguely remembered Lola's sweet voice telling me something about the zoo. The stillness and silence was perfect—so much activity and white noise had filled every day for months, it had been a long time since I'd felt such peace. I was gone, floating sound-free like a mime artist performing in space . . . until *clang!* Out came the north face of the Eiger. I went home to have a shower and drink 600 litres of water.

The Cath was making breakfast for Lola when I walked through the door. They both ran over and gave me a hug. I told them about Sid, that both he and Clare were doing well, but omitted the bit about giving birth to a mountain through my dick. 'Are you hungry?' The Cath asked.

I nodded and wandered off towards the bathroom. 'Jesus, what a night, mate,' said Jason after I told him why I was going to be late into the office. I threw the phone onto the bed and stripped on my way into the bathroom. We have one of those bathtub-shower combos so I climbed into the tub like an ancient man and turned on the shower taps. You can imagine the bliss.

As I stood there feeling safe, a little euphoric, but somewhat sore, squeezing shower gel into my hand and thinking about Sid and his mum coming home, the bathtub moaned at me. I dropped the shower gel and looked down. What the fuck? The tub groaned again then suddenly dropped, taking me and the shower curtain on a brief but exciting flight into the basement.

I lay there, still in the bath, the shower curtain twisted around me, smashed plaster and plastic pipes hanging above like giant spaghetti. My head hurt as I looked up at the light-filled hole above me, water pouring down on my face. Like an angel The Cath appeared in the light by the edge of the hole. 'Oh my god, Paul, Pauli, are you okay?'

'Yup,' I replied to the light. 'Turn off the water, will you, love?'

Slowly and cautiously moving one body part at a time, I got to my feet and realised I was unharmed. Wow, what a ride.

We found out later there was a small leak in the plumbing behind the taps in the wall cavity and over the years it had dripped away on the timber frame that held the bathtub in place. There was no substructure underneath the bath, as there should have been, so when the whole lot let go, it was catastrophic.

The Cath was there with a towel as I emerged, triumphant, from the basement. I called my insurance company and some tradies, and drank 600 litres of water.

ADVERTISING

TODAY IT'S SATURDAY and I'm once again stumbling through all the things I take for granted. The Saturday morning grocery shop, a truly horrendous experience, but not for the obvious reasons, like the first time I took Lola to the supermarket and blew all my money on smashed produce and ten packs of jelly, all because I put her in the trolley with the shopping instead of making her sit in the little seat. This time I'm on it; she's not smashing the eggs or randomly grabbing things off the shelves or sitting on the bread. This time she's in her seat and taking it all in, her soft, vulnerable brain a sponge for mass-marketing—my new fear.

In the past I've spent some time working in advertising, I know how it thinks, and it's clever. Marketers are trying to insert brands into my child's dreams, turn her into an obese TV junkie, kidnap her imagination and plaster giant logos across her soul. It's relentless and annoying. For example, all the chocolate bunnies that don't get sold at Easter get rewrapped in foil to look like Santa for Christmas.

Clare and I try to shield her mind from its reach and mostly she has been protected. Right now at the age of four, Lola likes to paint, dance, play in the garden; she likes the park and battering her little brother for no reason. She reads much more than she looks at the TV. In fact, she doesn't know how to turn on the TV or use the remote, and she has never been near the net. Suffice to say it will eventually trap her. We turn down the volume during commercial breaks when the networks turn it up, we avoid saying the names of particular stores that could entice a frenzy (we spell them out if we need to), we never go near junk food, and luckily she's afraid of clowns and equally suspicious of Santa.

But the mega-reach of the marketing machine has already touched her much more than I like. I start to pay attention to the cross-branding, realising I suddenly have half a dozen items in my trolley splattered in Toy Story crap. Lola sees and remembers everything: the Buzz Lightyear toilet plunger I just picked up or the Woody & Buzz shampoo—it goes on and on through every section of the supermarket.

She came home from day care last week demanding blonde hair because 'Barbie is blonde'. She does not have a Barbie doll, Barbie DVD or Barbie handgun, but thanks to the other kids at day care she is now familiar with the branding and wants to be a blonde. She's four. In the same week she discovered the computer, soon the internet will follow.

There are monsters under the bed, there are monsters under the packaging and behind every single website that ever existed. We unknowingly bring them into our homes and lives.

Think about it, but for all the right reasons, the ones you pretend not to think about until a random news story or article makes you remember. Indiscriminate and painful, the mother who can't start her child's heart because she didn't find the time to get the training, or that bastard who snatched a toddler from right under the father's distracted nose. Put faces on them, dead fractured faces. Without hesitation, without pause for reflection or consequences, I know I can become overprotective in a bad way, in a 'five to nine years but out in four for good behaviour' way. I'm not prone to violence, but I know it, like I know an alcoholic brother from a safe distance.

Clare is equally guarded and driven. That ability to fight, to protect, it's remarkable. I can tap into that protective rage like muscle memory.

It's a very, very bad world out there. I've seen human life sold for kicks and snuffed out for much less. I will have to educate my children extremely carefully; they are not growing up in poverty, they will not have to learn the hard way, like I did. Physical education in my day was more than pulling on a pair of what 70s Britain called 'plimsolls' and running around a muddy sports field. For my generation, physical education also often meant the back, or indeed the front, of your parent's hand. This is considered immoral and/or illegal in some places now, but that's how it was for many kids then. Besides, I couldn't beat the lessons into them anyway; it never worked for me. So how do I replicate the learning curve without destroying their innocence? Is it even possible? How do I teach my sprogs the value of their word, and the value of every dollar they make, and the value of life?

While I'm out doing the groceries I occasionally see things, triggers learnt over many years of being tuned in, usually men's eyes wandering over my family in a way that makes all my alarm bells ring. I feel the St Vitus dance vibrate through the floor, the airport travelator emerges through the frozen goods section ready to whisk me first class, at speed, via my gold ticket purchased years ago at the Slut Atlantic desk in Pakadaystan. Onward and upward into a shit-filled bloody broken explosion that would make Tarantino vomit in this lightly chilled flute of Cristal. Wonderful, isn't it? Being human, normal middle-class rules apply in Legoland malls, chew with your mouth closed and your mind open at all times. I can feel muffled screams, braille messages from behind the defunct veneers of happy family eyes . . . Just doing the shopping, home in time to get drunk and beat the lot of them senseless by dinnertime.

Get me out of here; sometimes the mall disturbs me more than Nigeria did.

CURRY

AFTER SPEED WEEK was cancelled in 2011 and the bike tested at Tailem Bend, we put her into storage and went back to our lives. For me, both businesses were doing well, our court case strolled on into more of the same redundant stalling and mesmerising drone. So we just rolled with it and paid the legal bills in the hope that the trial would be slated before another year went by.

Jason, though, was getting into it; our director was starting to read legal books and really listening to our QC in meetings. One morning when we were in the counsellor's office in the city I even caught him leaning in when the QC was talking.

'Fuck, you're keen,' I said as we grabbed a coffee in the huge marble-clad lobby during a break.

'I like it; it's like chess,' Jason countered.

'Yeah, do me a favour.'

'What?' He looked at me unblinkingly as he stirred sugar into his cup. 'I think it's amazing, court is fascinating.'

'So is my arsehole.'

We walked out into the sunlight with Jason expounding the virtues of the legal learning curve, how it was all a challenge, not a giant waste of time and money. 'You're just not interested in anything that doesn't have an engine or a gun involved,' he said, grinning.

I conceded this was true. In fact, while he'd been rabbiting on about the fascinations of law, my mind had drifted off and I was thinking about the salt.

'And stop drawing robots, for fuck's sake.'

In the end we all just got fed up paying the lawyers, I guess, and settled.

Ten months, three days and eight hours since I rode the BDM-SLS. (Give or take a few hours or days.) Spent largely doing nothing of significance whatsoever. Apart from Sid's arrival, I worked, changed nappies, went to swimming lessons, did the dishes, rode my motorcycle every day and slept well. My writing is uncomplicated and by implication my life can be very similar. Besides, I don't want to bore you with my normal activities and mortgage repayments.

This is how it went along until my phone rang. It was Colin—the time had come and our shot at Speed Week 2012 was upon us. And suddenly it was like a rising wave with about 400 other excitable bogans, emailing each other, cyber-chatting about the weather conditions, swapping tips (some very dodgy) on everything from air–fuel ratios and traction, to places to stay (I can recommend a gay-friendly motel), all preparing for our moment of salt-lake glory.

One of our first jobs was to get the bike through the final shakedown. This is the formal vetting and scrutineering of Speed Week vehicles at Tailem Bend test track by the Dry Lakes Racers Association. David Hinds and Peter Noy, two immensely likable gents from the DLRA, contacted me to organise the shakedown, and Colin, Rob, Ed and the uni lads dragged the bike out of storage and started prepping her. They had also redesigned and fixed the lifting issue, and made a few other modifications to finetune her performance. She was ready to roll.

I booked flights and the motel at Tailem Bend, then went to work like one of my robots while my mind opened up the heavily barricaded door that had been holding back an overflowing stream of salt-filled motorcycle dreams. The speed, the passionate lunatics I was going to meet and hopefully set records with. No matter what's going on in your life at the time, the moment you step onto the salt, breathe in the dry outback air, you're ready to leap on your bike or into your rocket-powered homemade car and smash it down the track as fast as

you can. Salt-lake racing crystallises the mind; it penetrated everything I was doing and I felt suddenly elated,
anticipation quickening my heart. All I wanted was my
shot down the track—I wanted to know if I could do it,
if the bike could do it, if it was the drug I thought it was.

My slow walk through the university grounds was
contemplative; I had done this several times before. As
I get older I'm prepared to accept that time does indeed
speed up, and, sure, there were periods when it felt like
Speed Week would never come, but, shit, now that I was
back I couldn't believe how fast the last year had gone by.
It was almost a carbon copy of the scene I walked into
one year ago, as I rounded the corner to see the same
faces packing the bike into the trailer—a Groundhog Day.

Colin muttered over his clipboard, Rob fiddled with
spare parts and Ed hovered around with his pants falling
off his arse. Ed has this look, and from the first time I met
him I started calling him 'Flock of Seagulls'. His thick
hair defies gravity without the aid of product, and has a
kind of retro-cool mid-80s Brit pop flair to it. He's like
a cross between Morrissey, Thomas Dolby and everyone
from Joy Division, except taller. Combine this look with
Ed's natural ability to remain slightly aloof but highly
aware of everything around him, and a good dose of
brilliance, and you've got a new-wave nutcase.

We rose early the next morning to a glorious warm
day. The drive from the uni to Tailem Bend was comfortable in the trailing final ebb of summer. We had a few
beers in the sun, a great curry at the pub, sitting on

the balcony overlooking the Murray River. Tomorrow clutch-in 7 a.m. sharp, this time without achieving flight. So it was off to my room above the pub which had a large window that looked onto the silver bend of the river through the small town. The sun had just set, leaving the last of the sparrows to dogfight aerobatics, chasing invisible bugs through the air in front of me. I fell into a deep restful summer Sunday night sleep.

Lightning woke me at 6 a.m. and I sat up to hear thunder and what sounded like the wind hurling dead sparrows against my window. I launched out of the bed, flinging the curtains aside and stood there naked and shocked. Before me was the exact opposite of yesterday's idyllic scene. Trees bent over against the wind, threatening to snap, the river void of happy water-skiers now raged angrily through the rain. I heard Colin next door fling his curtains open through the thin walls, followed by a clearly audible 'Fuck'. He was closely followed by Ed on the other side.

We met up in the car park in disbelief. 'Can you believe this?' Colin walked towards me his hands upturned. 'Every time we come here the weather turns to shit.'

I made agreeing noises but was inwardly focused on regretting that curry; it was repeating on me in a bad way.

We drove over to the roadhouse and had a slow breakfast. I ate dry toast and drank coffee in an effort to stop the curry from liquefying my tongue. Then I called David Hinds, and we agreed to go out to the track and hope for the weather to clear. David met us there with a few other DLRA members, and we all sat down and waited.

Meanwhile, David checked out my crotch and armpits, which isn't as nasty as it sounds. Not only does your bike get thoroughly checked at these shakedowns, the rider's gear has to pass safety standards, too. That year the DLRA adopted the US rules for the first time and one of the new rules stipulated that a rider's clothing had to be made entirely of leather. This caused a problem for many riders as modern motorcycle leathers have a stretchy elastic material in the gussets under the arms and often in the crotch area as well. These popular leathers don't comply with the new rules, which were probably established through the pain and suffering of some poor bastard who barbecued his ball sack when his bike burst into flames while doing 300 kph across the salt. So a compromise was offered in the form of a full-length fireproof underwear option. I pictured a large group of slightly overweight middle-aged men squeezed into knitted woollen body stockings and sucking in their guts for all they're worth while attempting to get the zip up on their already tight racing leathers, then passing out with heat exhaustion.

My racing leathers were given to me by my friend Erwin who had purchased them 30 years earlier, the first time he decided to see how fast he could go down a racetrack on a Ducati 900. They fit me well and are entirely made of leather so I have a fireproof crotch and armpits.

Finally the wind and rain died down and the track dried out a bit. I sat anxiously at the side of the track, watching David as he had a conversation with other DLRA members. Colin and the guys had the bike parked on the track and ready to pounce. Then David broke from his conversation, said something into his radio handset and lifted his head looking for me. I sprang from the side into his line of sight to get the nod.

Once again she burst to life under me and bolted down the track and through the gearbox, capping out at 170 kph, no eagles, no wobbles, no lifting. We were told at the start of the day that this exercise was not about speed but more about going over the bike, so I just eased down, turned her round in a huge arc (her battle-ship turning circle had not improved), and gunned her back to the pits.

My ride back was interrupted by the metabolic chain reaction of riding a fast but homemade experimental motorcycle down a racetrack after consuming a dodgy curry the night before, followed by coffee. As I leant forward to lie over the fuel tank, my brain put a bit too much effort into getting the gear changes right and forgot to maintain the clench and I passed what felt like a gram of gas. No problem, I thought, I can make it to the pits, get my leathers off and find a toilet before I lose my arse. Then it hit me. The tiny fart had expanded into a cubic metre of horrendous air that rose sharply up through my leathers and filled my helmet. I gagged, my eyes stung, the bike was passing 160 kph, I sat up and flipped open my visor in a desperate effort to breathe fresh air, nearly crashing when the wind hit my open lid and tried to rip my head off my shoulders.

Pulling up fast I leapt off, handed the bike to the boys and ran off pointing at the toilet block. Our bike passed the shakedown with flying colours, so did my curry.

That was it; everything was prepped, organised, checked, approved and ready to go. All we had to do now was wait for Speed Week to kick off in a fortnight.

SPEED WEEK 2. 2012

I WAS WALKING down a tree-lined street near the city towards my motorcycle having just left a meeting. It was lunchtime and West Perth was awash with business people rushing about and packing the most into one hour out of the office. Crossing the street, wondering if I got a parking ticket, past a busy al fresco restaurant, I felt my phone buzz in my pocket. It was just past 1 p.m. on Friday, 9 March.

'Hi, Paul, it's David Hinds here.' As soon as I heard his voice I stopped walking and closed my eyes. 'Have I caught you at a bad time?'

'No,' I lied, as my mind raced through his reasons for calling me and instantly deduced that whatever his reason it was not a good thing.

'Mate, I'm so sorry to have to tell you this, but Speed Week is officially canc—'

'*Fuuuuuuucckk! Noooooooo!*' At least half the diners jumped as I cut David off, dropped the phone and my helmet, tried to kick it and missed, which is really embarrassing and extra infuriating because when you miss on a big kick and totally disconnect in rage, the momentum will tear muscles and send your body into the air in a banana-skin slip that ends with a very sore tail bone.

Then, as I rolled onto my chest and tried to stand up, I put my palms down on the pavement pinning my neck tie and that choked me slightly, so the rage diverted to a high-speed tie-removal throat disco that went on for entirely too long.

At some point I became aware of stillness and stopped my thrashing to discover that every single person around me was staring. One woman was filming me on her iPhone. I felt my head turn purple. I picked up my phone and helmet and walked straight to the nearest bar.

So one week away from the start of Speed Week and it was cancelled again for the second year. The rain had lashed down over the preceding few days, putting 8 inches of water on top of the salt. The Dry Lakes Racers officials had made the huge effort of regularly going out to the lake and checking its condition, only to return with the sad news. Faced with the amount of water and the knowledge that it would not dissipate and dry up in time, they had no choice but to cancel.

I sat at the bar plying myself with whiskey and going over the options. There was no way I was giving up. Sure, as a backup plan we could just go back to Tailem Bend, but it was a desperately close call on whether the bike could get the record there—the track's only 1.4 k's long, and we'd have to make considerable changes to the bike then have it re-scrutineered by the officials.

I needed more room, a minimum of 2 kilometres, I needed somewhere that was flat and safe and legal, and I needed it now.

My problem was time, I was on a deadline. The bike was part of the university curriculum, a subject matter for the students to learn from. Its whole conception was based on creating a motorcycle for salt-lake racing from nothing. That was now achieved and the next wave of students would soon be reinventing the bike into a hovercraft or submarine or something. My two-year window was closing fast.

And, of course, many lives had been planned around the dates for Speed Week: everyone had taken time off work, bookings had been made, all the many and varied components built around this five-day period. They'd all be disappointed, too.

First I decided I needed to call Doug Gould. He was supplying the speed data logging equipment and this kit was paramount. So I finished my whiskey, ordered another and picked up the phone. Doug and I talked through the options. His business is tracking speed, so he knows every place with potential; he is also a pilot so he knows more than a few airstrips as well. We spent the afternoon on the phone working our way through all possible sites but, despite how big our continent is, we ended up with a very short list. It turned out that our options were limited because of the timeframe and the length of track we needed.

While I was on the phone to Doug, the DLRA had been busy, too. They had somehow come up with permission to get onto Lake Gairdner between 28 May and 1 June, on a different part of the lake, one that was dry. Getting the permission to do this kind of thing is in a word gargantuan; there are so many people to convince, government departments to lobby, councils to liaise with, environmental regulations to adhere to, it goes on and on. But the DLRA are a determined bunch and had managed to shift the parameters for a second attempt at holding Speed Week. A massive effort by the guys. Not only that, but they'd also gone out to Lake Omeo in the Victorian High Country and secured it as a backup location. Of course, while they were at Lake Omeo organising the second site, 9 inches of rain pelted down; it had not rained like that in ten years, the lake was underwater.

So I was sitting in a bar looking at a very short list, distilled like my whiskey down through many stages. We had checked every possible option, every airport runway, private roads, private council roads, military roads, mud lakes, other salt lakes, anything and everything we thought we could run the bike on. In the end I left

Doug to chase down the list and went home; he had the contacts to make the calls and I had to get ready for a work trip to Brisbane in the morning.

My flight the next day cruelly took me over Lake Gairdner. Again I pressed my nose up against the perspex window and peered down at the water, but instead of my usual excitement and anticipation, I felt hopeless. I was really starting to think that I just wasn't meant to be doing this.

Gregg Cooper was sitting next to me; we do a lot of business together, he's a perpetual 'can do' man. He laughed as I snivelled out the window.

'Bonneville,' he said. 'You need to go stateside.'

He was talking about the mecca of salt-lake racing, Bonneville in Utah, where it all began. Bonneville Speed Week was held annually in September, and attracted the craziest of the crazies. 'Of course an American's going to tell me that,' I replied moodily. 'But we're flying over a perfectly good salt lake right fuckin' now.'

'Lake being the operative word there, Pauli.'

I gazed down at the water. Yep, my racetrack was a lake. 'It's not going to work, mate,' I said. 'I wouldn't have enough time to get the bike to Bonneville.'

Gregg narrowed his eyes at me in a no-bullshit way. 'So figure it out, man, make it happen.'

Gregg's from Texas, he's like that. When he came to Australia six years ago from Houston to start his own oil and gas supply business, he had very little. No contacts, no leg up the Aussie food chain, but he

nailed it. How? Because he walked into a market domi-
nated by old-school back-scratching slack-arse 'Nah,
mate, some other time' attitudes. He had more drive and
motivation than his local competition, and deservedly
did well. Right now, though, he was turning that deter-
mination on me, and giving me plenty to think about.

We landed in Brisbane, jumped in a cab and headed
for the hotel. Gregg had booked a massive self-catering
top-floor penthouse bang in the middle of the city. It's
one of the things I like about Gregg and Maximum
Dave, who was joining us on this trip. These are men
with drive and direction, always that one step ahead
of the game in business. MD can see the angle like a
pool shark feigning a defeat, then he strikes. I know if
I sawed off the top of MD's head his fiendishly designed
brain would glow incandescent and powerful. These
two always do things on the top shelf. They just don't
travel unless they can lavish a high level of hedonism
into it. Dave is all about turning left when he gets on
an aircraft, and Gregg is a gastronomic genius, so even
though I'm usually content to travel rough, if I'm on a
business trip with these guys I happily raise my bar and
put on three kilos in a week.

Take, for example, the dinner arrangements for that
evening. An acclaimed restaurant within walking distance
from our opulent digs, the house speciality was aged
beef, the wine list was world-class, the decanters crystal,
a waiter rushed up with a tiny dustpan and broom to
remove crumbs from the table as I tore into my bread

roll, the toilet was way better appointed than my house, and the maître d' was so efficient he had to be a cyborg. Meanwhile, the three of us are bouncing the steel ball of business angles, fart jokes and banter like an oilfield pinball machine that got delivered to the wrong hotel.

Suddenly I started sweating, then I got dizzy, really dizzy. I loosened my tie and gulped water.

'You okay, mate?' Gregg asks. His brow is furrowed and the look on his face tells me that I'm not okay at all.

I attempted to stand up and vaguely remember telling him to get me back to the room. Which he did, because I woke up on the floor in the penthouse bathroom. And immediately started vomiting, hard.

Gregg put a blanket around me and told me an ambulance was on its way. 'Holy shit, man, I haven't seen puking like that since I was in college.'

I couldn't raise my head and blacked out again.

In the ambulance, vomiting at light speed, it was like the devil himself had his arm down my throat and was squeezing my stomach as hard as he could. I was sweating so much my clothes were soaking wet. The paramedic was yelling at me above the siren while slapping my face, someone was pouring water on my head and another was holding a bag over my mouth. I was scared, really scared. I fought hard to take in what was happening around me but I just couldn't focus on anything. Then I was out again.

Next time I woke up in a hospital room—again. I had spent more time in hospital in the past year than

I had in my entire life, including being born. 'Kidney stone?' I asked as the doctor walked in.

He looked puzzled. 'No, it looks like you have an inner ear infection that caused a violent and acute attack of vertigo.'

To me, vertigo is an Alfred Hitchcock movie or the U2 album, not a face-planting sweaty vomit-filled trip to the hospital. But apparently that's exactly what vertigo can do. I was very wobbly on my feet for the next two days, with no sense of direction or which way was up and I couldn't focus; it was a very strange thing to experience and all because I picked up an ear infection, probably from my own children. It's another joy of parenting: your carrier monkeys bring home enough parasites, bacteria and general nasty infectious shit to start a zombie plague.

Which brings me to Maximum Dave and our flight back to Perth.

The whole cabin was spinning, I was nauseous, the in-flight meal smelt like a decomposing body, and my elementary canal started to go into spasm. Then Dave pulled the earphones from his head, spun his laptop screen at me, pointed to the paused frame of a female zombie with breast implants and joyfully declared she was a ZILF. That was the end of me. I vomited into the in-flight magazine and not the bag that was supposed to be there.

'Can I eat your lunch then?' asks Maximum Dave.

'Choke on it, motherfucker.' I had four more hours of this to get through.

I'd lost two days, one spent in the hospital, the other in a dark hotel room. When we landed in Perth I turned on my phone as we wandered down the escalator towards the luggage carousel—I nearly had a nervous breakdown as 200-plus emails and messages flooded in.

DIEGO

BECAUSE ANY TRIP out of Perth to the east coast chews up a day in travel, I had effectively been away for four days. In this time, Doug had managed to get a tentative yes from just one place on our list—the Corowa Airport near Albury-Wodonga on the border of Victoria and New South Wales. Apart from being the only option that suited our timeframe, and the only place that was amenable to our far-fetched plans, Corowa is well laid out with a 2-kilometre main runway and 200 metres of grass runoff in every direction.

In the back of the cab on the way home from the airport as I scanned through the backlog of emails and messages, blatantly disregarding anything that wasn't bike-related, I got a snapshot of Doug's amazing feats over the past few days while I'd been wobbling around with vertigo: the Corowa airport management team had agreed; Doug was working on the local council; because the airport was being closed that week for the army to train their parachute display team, we needed to get the official permission from the army as well. It was Thursday, and all this had to happen by Monday, when we would have a one-hour window between eight and nine in the morning to use the main runway. Fuck me, it was going to be tight.

I went straight into planning mode and called the guys at the uni to get the ball rolling on a plan to get there. I sent Colin the map of the airport runway, he came back to me straightaway, saying it would be a close call but the runway should be long enough.

There was so much to do in so little time.

First, we had to have the runway surface checked, get the insurance in place, a risk assessment including medical personnel, fire team, full radio comms monitoring with any aircraft that needed to come in, the speed data logging equipment and of course we still needed the army to give us the nod. That worried me because from my experiences with the defence forces there is a system, the chain of command, and I was sure they had much more important things to be focusing on than our bike run. But the following day the army—bless them—came straight back with a big fat 'No Worries' and by lunchtime it was all squared away for Monday, 19 March.

The guys at the uni had the bike ready in the trailer and I had sorted out the accommodation in Corowa. That's when I decided it would be fun to get my bike shipped over to Adelaide so I could ride to Corowa, then after the land-speed attempt I could ride down to Melbourne and get smashed with Clayton Jacobson. Picture a man who looks like he just ate an entire roast chicken without using his hands; he's a big man, not in a fat way, but in a big man, big beard, big hair, big sense of humour way. I knew if I stayed over at Clay's place I would then jump on the ferry the next day with a hangover and spend a week riding around Tasmania sobering up only to do it again on the way home. I didn't make it to Tassie when I went around Australia on Betty the baby-faced-killer motorcycle two years ago so, hey, why not do it now?

My bike-riding mate Diego is from Argentina, so he's extremely well mannered, very dark and handsome, always well dressed and groomed, has a ridiculously big, charismatic smile and speaks with a bog-thick South American accent. You know, the sort that makes women glaze over with mental images of being undressed by Antonio Banderas. I see a guy who sounds and dresses like the cat from *Shrek* and is about the same size too.

I was grabbing a quick lunch break with Diego and filling him in on all the latest happenings with the bike run. He was stuffing his wife's empanadas from a lunchbox into his face. The wonderful aroma brought back memories of the first time I met Diego's wife, Veronica, and her amazing empanadas. They were coming over to our place and earlier that day Clare had asked me to move Sid to the other end of the table, so I picked him up, high chair and all, twisted, leant and bent over, putting my back out and writhing in pain on the floor while Lola berated me for using all the bad words at once. I crawled to the bathroom on my stomach, grabbed some pills leftover from a bike stack I had a few years before and all was fine. Diego and Veronica arrived with the empanadas. She was gorgeous and gracious, of course, and I attempted to extend every gentlemanly courtesy, but on 40 milligrams of morphine, I actually appeared mentally incompetent or psychopathic or both. I could not stop eating the empanadas; needless to say the evening was fun for me and a disaster for Clare. Anyway, since then I've been addicted to Veronica's empanadas.

So back to Diego who, having demolished half a dozen, was grinning at me like a well-fed hamster. 'Pol, can I come wid you, my friend?'

'Well, yeah, course you can, mate, but we're riding hard all day every day, so no mincing about, no grinning or hanging around like an extra from a pirate movie.'

'Pol, wat are you talking about?' He looked genuinely puzzled as he flicked a speck of pastry off his Hugo Boss sleeve then flashed a grin at a random passerby.

Several phone calls the next day had all the guys

who were coming with us to Speed Week diverting to Corowa instead. Simon and Howard both decided to ride their bikes down from Brisbane. Simon was on an antique BMW R60 and Howard was riding a Buell he had managed to load up with enough gear to make it look more like a Pakistani mule. Also on the way was Brendan, my photographer mate. At the time he was running about in the outback trying to get a picture of some ultra-elusive native nocturnal bird. Brendan's not into birdwatching, he'd rather set fire to his underpants than creep about in the bush at night, but as soon as some muppet told him no one's ever captured it on film he was off like Bear Grylls after a juicy grub.

Then I started the phone calls to get both Diego's and my bike on freight to Adelaide. This is when I discovered that I had missed my window for road freight out of Perth to Adelaide by one day. So I tried the train, no dice, and alternate routes, no time, so I called some specialty bike transport companies.

'Where from?' they asked.

'Perth.' I held my breath.

'Forget it,' they said.

So then I thought about riding over, but my fuel tank is too small, so I considered hiring a ute, putting the bikes on it and driving them over myself, but that just sounded silly. So I called a friend, Ashley Taylor, who runs Pentagon Freight.

'You're a lucky bastard,' he said. And I was. Ash had a truck leaving Perth for Adelaide the day after tomorrow, and there was just enough room on the back to put two bikes. There was only one hitch: we had to put the bikes in crates.

So I called the companies that make crates to order, but there was either no time, no response to messages or no actual sense of effort. That meant I was going to have to build the crates myself. Erwin called me from a rig somewhere in the South China Sea while I was on my way to the timber yard to ask how it was all panning out. I got as far as explaining the crates when he laughed. 'Shit, Pauli, you're a dumb arse,' said the man who was, to me, like a brother, mentor, friend and Yoda.

'Well, fuck you, too, champ,' I barked.

He chuckled, which annoyed me even more. 'What kind of bike is Diego riding?'

'A new BMW 650 Tourer,' I replied curtly.

'Mate, call up the Harley and BMW dealers in Perth and ask for a shipping crate. I guarantee they'll have crates out the back purpose-built for both your bikes.' And this is why the man is a legend.

The next morning Diego and I met at Pentagon Freight, put our bikes into the crates and booked our flights to Adelaide. He was arriving a few hours ahead of me, so he would go to the freight yard and run the bikes over to our motel. I would arrive and meet with the uni team to go over the plan for getting to Corowa. Everything was set.

I drove home from Pentagon feeling like there was a good viable plan in place to counter the loss of everything so far—Speed Week 1, Jocko, my Ural, all of it. The plan covered a lot of distance and was on a ridiculous time-frame with no room for error. Our bikes would arrive in Adelaide the day before Diego and I, we'd get them fuelled up and ready to go, then get the salt-lake bike ready for an early departure from Ed's workshop. It was a ten-hour ride to Corowa, then at 6 a.m. on Monday we'd set up the bike at the runway, break a world record between 8 and 9 a.m. and by lunchtime Diego and I would be on the freeway headed for Melbourne. We would have to skip getting drunk with Clayton to catch the 4 p.m. ferry to Tassie. Easy.

Friday night my phone rang. It was Mick, one of the blokes from Pentagon Freight. 'Hi Paul, I've got some bad news,' he said.

I was walking out of my local deli with a carton of milk and a bottle of tomato sauce. I froze mid-stride; I didn't want to ask but I had to. 'What sort of bad news?'

'Yeah, well, you see, somehow your bikes were loaded onto the wrong truck and are on their way to Karratha.'

'FUUUUUUCCCKKKK!' I dropped the milk. 'WHADYA FUCKIN' MEAN KARRATHA?'

There was a brief silence while Mick regained his hearing. 'Don't worry, we're on top of it,' he hurriedly explained. 'We've got the Karratha truck pulled over and the Adelaide truck pulled over, we're mobilising up a long tray ute with a pallet jack to pick up your bikes then we'll hotshot them over to the Adelaide truck. They'll get there, but about twelve hours late.'

Which meant the bikes would arrive in Adelaide just a few hours before we did. That would still work. I thanked Mick, asked him to keep in touch, picked up my carton of milk, smiled sweetly at the other customers who avoided eye contact with me, and went home to spend time with my family.

KEYS

THAT AFTERNOON I jumped on the flight to Adelaide. Start the clock.

Diego had been on the phone as soon as he landed. The bikes had arrived at exactly the same time he did and he had already ridden his bike over to the motel and was heading back on mine, via Ed's workshop to take a gander at the BDM-SLS. I told him to leave my bike there as we were all heading off from the workshop in the morning; he could double me on his bike from the hotel.

Ed's workshop is cool. He lives there with two of his mates, Simon and Tristan, all recently graduated from the University of Adelaide. Casual but not chaotic, in fact rather polished and well-engineered, it's the ultimate man cave. All three of the guys had been involved with the BDM–SLS from its inception and in many ways their careers have evolved like the bike, now out in the world looking to make a mark.

Diego and I finally met up outside the motel; I had just dumped my gear in my room and he was walking towards me, grinning the way only he can. 'Heello, my friend,' he said, beaming just like the cat from *Shrek*.

'Good work, mate,' I said, squeezing him in a blokey hug. Our motel was at the busy end of Hindley Street, Adelaide's epicentre of nightlife. It was 6 p.m. on Saturday, 17 March and the sun was about to depart, leaving the neon and noise to take over, and already the street was awash with pissed idiots in various shades of green clothing and drinking green beer.

'What ees going on, Pol?' Diego gesticulated, palms up and confused face, at the green-clad drunks.

'It's St Patrick's Day, mate,' I replied. Right on cue a particularly hammered guy in green coveralls staggered out of a bar and walked straight into a lamppost and face-planted on the street.

'Who ees this saint? Why ees everybody drunk?'

I paused. How do I start to explain our lust for any excuse to have a day off work and hit the piss? Diego doesn't get our sports, our humour or the sometimes blatantly racist things we say without thinking. 'You hungry?' I ask him.

'No,' he answered, still scanning the street in amazement.

I was in desperate need of a shower so Diego and I arranged to meet back at the motel; he said he'd take half an hour to check out some sunglasses he'd seen in a shop (if I spent more than half a minute choosing sunglasses I might have some style, too).

Showered up and happy, I was back out the front of the motel, just checking out the scene while I waited for Diego—it was party time now and the street was packed with punters. Then I saw him running towards me like someone just stole the family empanada recipe. 'Pol, Pol . . . I can't believe eet . . . Eet cannot be possible . . .' he gasped. He was really agitated, and frantically going through his jacket pockets.

'What the fuck is it, mate?'

His dark Argentinean eyes fixed on me, his expression bewildered and gutted. 'I have lost the keys to both our motorcycles.'

'*Fuuuuccccckkkk!*' was my immediate reaction before I calmed down and fired all the standard questions at him, you know, when did have them last, have you retraced your steps, gone back to the shop and asked the staff, would you like me to kill you slowly or just hurt you badly. But they were gone, properly gone, lost on Hindley Street. And of course Diego had checked everywhere already.

We went to the police station, ironically directly across the street, and gave our details to the cop behind the counter in case someone handed the keys in. He smiled and reached under the counter to produce a bucket full of keys. 'No worries. If they end up here, we'll let you know.'

The problem solidified in my head like a cement tumour as I sat down on the kerb next to Diego's bike. He dropped down next to me like he was bearing the weight of the known universe on his shoulders. 'Pol, wat are we going to do now?'

It was 7 p.m. on a Saturday night, St Patrick's Day, we had no keys for our bikes and we were due out of there in eleven hours for our one and only shot at the land-speed record. There were spare keys at both our homes in Perth, but no time to get them to us. 'I need a drink.'

'Good idea, Pol.' Diego sprang to his feet and disappeared into the bar while I sat on the kerb staring at the road, oblivious to the rambling hordes all around me, not really focusing on anything but searching blankly through the options. I could smell the whiskey before I realised it was under my chin; Diego was back on the kerb with two large glasses.

We slammed down our drinks and my brain kicked into gear. Okay, I thought, so Diego's bike is here right next to me, it's not alarmed and the steering lock isn't engaged; my bike's in Ed's workshop, it is alarmed but the alarm control is cable-tied to the handlebars so the movement of the transport truck wouldn't set it off, it also has an un-engaged steering lock . . . so our only problem was replacing the ignition keys. All I had to do was find a locksmith on a Saturday night who wasn't drunk (that discounted the Irish ones) with the right blank keys to fit a Harley Sportster and a new BMW GS and convince him to stop whatever he was doing and fix our problem. Easy.

Diego searched for locksmiths on his phone and, faking a smile, left me with a list while he went to get more drinks. The first two didn't answer, the third was already smashed, the fourth and fifth sent me on one of those daisy-chain circles where the phone is answered by a machine that directs you to call another number that directs you to another machine that rings a mobile for you, so you can listen to another machine asking you to leave a message or tell you about their normal office hours, or the best one, getting diverted back to the first machine that kicks off the whole process again. The sixth number just took me to a recorded message by some twat about his pissy-ass weekend fishing trip and he wouldn't be back to fix fuck all until Monday. One guy nearly gave in: he was obviously out at the pub and close to starting his third or fourth beer, he paused to reflect after I tripled his asking price. 'Nah, mate, can't help ya, sorry.'

Staring despondently at Diego, a light bulb went off. 'You're an educated man, Diego, you have a masters degree in mechanical engineering from one of the best universities in Argentina.'

'Yes, I do,' he said proudly.

'Can you hotwire a bike?' The solution was so simple, so obvious, so desperate.

His brow furrowed like a cat who's caught a sniff of something. 'I weel try, let us go to the shed of Ed and I weel get some toolings.'

My phone rang as we finished off our third whiskeys and were leaving to steal our own bikes. 'Is that Paul?' said the voice on the other end. 'It's Ben from Australian Locksmiths here.'

'Hi Ben, are you out and/or on the piss and calling to tell me that you can fix my problem on Monday?'

There was a pause. 'No, sir, I'm calling you back to see what can we do for you tonight.'

Hope rising, I was almost too scared to say the next bit. 'Ben, can you cut a key for a 2011 Harley Davidson Sportster and a 2011 BMW 650 GS before six tomorrow morning?'

'Where are you?' he asked.

'I'm on the corner of Gilbert Place and Hindley Street outside the pub.'

'Yeah, I know the place,' said Ben. 'Just hang on while I check our stock.'

Diego was gesticulating madly doing his Argentinean pantomime of 'What the fuck's going on' while I pointed at the phone and pantomimed back.

'Paul,' Ben's voice returned and both Diego and I froze mid-mime. 'We have plenty of blanks to fit your Sportster and just one blank left that will fit the BMW. I could be there in thirty minutes if you like.'

'Shit hot, Ben!' I thanked him, we exchanged a few details and I put my phone in my pocket. 'We're good, mate,' I said to Diego, who was bouncing around so happily I thought he was going to have a seizure. 'He's on the way.'

'This ees wonderful, Pol.' Diego's grin had returned. 'I will get us some green beer,' he said and rushed off to the bar again.

Ben was there, right on time; he had a van with a kind of mini lathe thing in the back and basically in one fell swoop destroyed my faith in the lock and key. He looked over Diego's bike then stuck what looked like a magic wand with a flashlight on it into the slot where the key goes. Diego was fascinated, 'Ben, wat dos dis thing do?'

Ben was very polite and explained he was taking measurements so he could build up a picture of what the key should look like. 'Oh, I have a photo of my bike key on my phone,' Diego said. 'Would that help?'

Diego had grown up riding bikes with his mates all over his father's property. The bikes they had were old and in a perpetual near-death state held together with hope and gaffer tape. As a kid he never dreamt he would one day walk into a BMW dealership and purchase outright a new bike off the showroom floor. Diego was so excited at the prospect of having a bike that started with the use of a key and electronic ignition, instead of a lot of kicking and praying, that he took a photo of the key to show his pals back home.

Ben looked at the photo, said 'Perfect,' and disappeared into his van, emerging about fifteen minutes later with a key that slid into Diego's ignition and turned the bike over on the first try.

'Amazing,' said Diego over his green beer. 'Ben, can you defeat any lock?'

'So far,' said Ben.

'Sheet hot,' said Diego.

Then I jumped on the back of Diego's bike and we rode the few k's over to Ed's workshop with Ben following in his magic van. Ed was there with Simon and Tristan and they all laughed hard at our situation. While Ben went to work on my ignition with his magic wand, I moaned to Simon about the fact that along with my bike key I had also lost the padlock key which secured my saddlebags to the bike. While nodding and listening Simon casually pulled a small leather ziplock case from his backpack, wandered over and glanced at my bike, opened his leather case, selected two steel lock picks from within, and 30 seconds later both of the so-called unpickable padlocks were off.

'Where did you learn how to do that?' I was stumped.

Ben acknowledged Simon's effort with a nod.

'Sheet hot,' said Diego.

Ben was done within the hour, and not only could I start my bike but I had two extra keys in case history repeated on me, so I later stitched one into the top of my riding boot and put the other on a string around my neck. It was almost 10 p.m. by the time our superhero locksmith left, with me calling out, 'I love you, Ben.' Diego was not feeling the love; he was paying the $1400 bill that Ben just handed him.

Ed ordered a pizza and produced a six-pack of beer; by midnight everyone was full and happy, and every bike was ready for clutch-in at 6 a.m., destination Corowa some ten hours and 900 kilometres away. Diego and I grabbed a cab back to the motel. Hindley Street looked like a big-production zombie movie was being made, the premise of which involved a storyline based on the entire population of Adelaide being infected and turning into green-beer-swilling shuffling corpses for which the cure was apparently Hungry Jacks.

JACK
THE
DANCER

IT WAS STILL dark outside at 5.30 that morning. I sat on my backpack at the corner where the alleyway that housed our motel met Hindley Street and surveyed the St Patrick's Day carnage through the clouds of fog my breath billowed into the darkness. The odd zombie still staggered about in the middle distance looking for food.

Diego would be down shortly and our adventure would kick off. I checked my phone for emails and messages; there was one missed call last night from my dad in the UK. By the time Diego arrived my world had changed. He stopped where I sat, squatting down in front of me and smiling at first as he asked what I was doing. My face was blank; I found his eyes and saw his happy expression fade away. He watched me trying to find the words, any words, and waited, hovering there in limbo while rhythmical clouds floated skyward.

'My dad's got cancer,' I finally said. 'It's serious, but he'll know more later in the week after he's had surgery.'

Diego sat down next to me and suddenly words poured out uncontrollably as I rambled, about my dad, about getting to the UK to be with him as soon as possible—all my plans including Corowa didn't rate a mention anymore. I could have sat there talking about it all day but then our cab pulled up. The driver and Diego spoke briefly, my friend occasionally glancing at me still sitting on the corner. Diego threw his backpack into the boot and walked back to me.

'Pol, your father would like to see you do this, eh?' He nodded towards the cab behind him and extended his hand towards me.

I focused on Diego's face for a moment, his eyes unwavering. I grabbed his hand and got myself together.

An hour later we were pulling away from Ed's workshop in convoy. Associate Professor Colin Kestell, mechanical legend Robert Dempster and Ed were in the university vehicle, a V8 Holden, pulling the giant custom-made trailer that cocooned the bike, followed by Diego and me riding our bikes.

I sat at the back, my head burbling along on auto-pilot, thinking about my father and what he must be going through. I suspected he had kept his illness from me for some time, being the type who prefers not to burden his offspring with worries, but was now forced to tell us that he was facing an abyss. When we spoke he had been as resolute as ever, but I could feel the hollow unspoken rattle of doubt over the distance, a distance my heart wanted to cross now. As we passed through the outskirts of Adelaide, I saw a sign for the airport and I had to fight the urge to just peel off and get on a plane. But I knew that if I suddenly pulled the pin and fronted up at my father's place, he'd just call me a muppet.

Before I knew it we had stopped in Tailem Bend and right on cue, the second I toed out my kickstand, the sky turned dark with ominous-looking clouds. We had some breakfast and talked about the journey ahead. Putting a call in to Howard and Simon revealed they had ridden into some heavy weather already as they tracked down towards Corowa from Brisbane. Brendan, who'd been out god-knows-where near Broken Hill chasing that mythical bird, had also pulled up because of rough weather. Ed got onto his phone straightaway to check out the weather sites and confirmed we were probably going to hit a massive front making its way down the entire eastern seaboard.

I know I'm not at all tech-savvy: the use of computers as a business tool is only seven years old to me, and I got my first mobile phone at 30, reluctantly. While several friends and colleagues swear by their smartphones, I'm embarrassed to say I struggle to use the Blackberry my business demands I carry around. But the ease with which Ed checked the weather bamboozled me.

I am usually the first to declare how appalling technology has made our ability to retain everyday slithers of information. My generation grew up without the internet or mobile phones, and we could remember everything; I can still pull up all my friends' numbers, their birthdays and addresses, old passport numbers, bank account details in foreign countries, the lot. But in conversation with a twenty-something, it's all gone; a twenty-something with a Mensa digit IQ and a masters in mechanical engineering has grown up in a system that remembers everything for him. We have outsourced memory and are forgetting how to remember. We can remember lots of different ways to access information quickly and little else for everyday life. I would imagine the education system these days is based on little of what I experienced; in my time, ironically, education was all about memory, the repetitive recall of spelling, multiplication tables, capital cities, the Latin word for shit. I believe that a good old-fashioned suitably absorbent memory gives you the platform for the production of creative ideas. While I'm riding my bike, doing the dishes or sitting in interminable legal meetings, I can wander off into my thoughts and memories and circumvent the now.

But with Ed tracking the weather by the minute and Diego looking at his iPhone, which is telling him where he is, how far he has to go, how long it will take, and who is emailing, texting, phoning and generally thinking about him in real time, I suddenly felt left out. I want to join the Steve Jobs club and face-plant my wife or let random strangers know that I don't like peanut butter on Twatter or whatever it's called.

The rain really kicked in as the convoy drove away from Tailem Bend—Diego and I had to stop to get our wet weather gear on and, despite his heated grips, his hands were so frozen I lent him my racing gloves—but it gave way to sunshine as we threaded through the rolling green hills, passed Pinnaroo and crossed over the border of South Australia and into Victoria. I tried not to think about my dad, or leaving my own remains scattered over a bit of Corowa Airport's main runway the next day.

Another fuel stop and phone call to Howard and Simon. The news wasn't good: Simon had turned back, but Howard was pushing on. Howard is a great rider, albeit somewhat mental. A few years ago he was out alone on a quiet country back road on a Sunday morning; always curious about what's over the next crest or round the next corner, honing his skills, finding that sweet spot when it all falls into place, he rode along in a trance—so far that he actually crossed the state border—and eventually came undone on the way home and stacked, though he walked away without a scratch. I saw his helmet sitting in the corner of his garage, the entire front half was ground away as he slid down the road on his face.

So anyway, Howard is capable of seriously hard riding and I could hear a storm in the background as he yelled excitedly into the phone. 'I've never ridden in rain like this, mate. I'm at a truck stop in Murwillumbah, had to stop, the vis is, like, 30 feet, and there's so much water on the road my bike's aquaplaning . . .'

'Fuck that!' I tried to tell him not to push it, that it wasn't worth the risk.

'Bollocks, I'll see you in Corowa,' and with that he hung up.

Brendan was out of reach with no mobile reception so I left a couple of messages. I could only hope he would make it; without his talent there would be no decent photos.

Colin and Ed had been on their iPhones. 'Call Howard back and tell him to stop and turn around,' Colin said. There was major flooding all around the area he was about to try to ride through. But of course Howard wasn't answering. I pictured him atop his heavily laden Buell, tucked in behind the fairing getting pummelled, and felt awful.

Especially because we were now travelling in perfectly balmy, sunny weather and really starting to enjoy the ride. At one point I pulled over and Colin hopped on my bike for a bit, then Ed had a go, then I jumped on Diego's bike and he on mine. His bike is everything you would expect for an uber-engineered German motorcycle—quiet, reliable, very comfortable, plenty of power, whether you're on a freeway or up a mountain. It's shaft-driven with an ingenious rear-swing arm system and an equally clever adjustable suspension and steering dampening design that can be altered without the use of tools. It's got huge luggage panniers that can be collapsed or expanded in seconds to house everything from a pair of socks to the kitchen sink, heated grips and seat so your hands and botty are always snug, a front fairing that deflects the wind and rain away from the rider, and mounting brackets for your GPS, iPhone and bike-to-bike comms system. It tells you how far it can travel on the remaining fuel, what your average fuel consumption is, how the engine is doing, how the oil is feeling, if the tyres are pumped to be here today. It will call ahead, introducing itself as Günter from Dusseldorf, book your dinner table not too close to the toilets and facilitate your hotel reservations, making sure the turndown maid leaves a rose on the pillow next to a card that will of course read 'Love always, Günter'.

My Harley does none of those things. It hurls the riding experience in your face and through your body like a backhander from an angry 6-foot chain-smoking Milwaukee kickboxer. But that's why I love it so much: it's unsophisticated, uncomplicated and a joy to ride.

We had a ball swapping vehicles over the next few hours, but the best part for me was seeing the facial expressions of the guys as they climbed off my bike. Compared to the loving backward glance always delivered to Diego's BMW, the reaction on dismounting my bike was more akin to one of pensioners who just got off a rollercoaster and are relieved they didn't soil themselves.

'Oh bloody hell, that was fun,' said Colin, 'but I've had enough.' He handed me back my open-face helmet that just intensifies the experience.

By mid-afternoon we were in Piangil on the Victorian and New South Wales border, drinking coffee and going through the routine of fuelling up, peeing and making phone calls. Howard picked up; he sounded deflated and was holed up in a motel room in Ballina. 'Sorry, man, I'm not gonna make it. It's too full-on.'

I could tell he was a bit pissed off with himself at the realisation he was riding beyond his internal safety warning system. This system is genetically hardwired into a man's brain box and turns itself on when we have kids; it only goes off when it senses near-death situations that don't involve protecting your wife and kids. No doubt Howard's had gone off in his head while he was sliding his Buell sideways down a flooded road in a thunderstorm.

Howard had already made a massive effort to be there last year when we ran the bike at Tailem Bend after Speed Week was cancelled, and this time he had loaded up his bike with 50 pounds of kit and ridden flat-out at the drop of a hat in the worst conditions imaginable to try to be there again. While I appreciated every effort, I was relieved that he'd made the wise choice.

'I really wanted to go round Tassie and hit it hard,' he said.

There was a pause while I paced circles in the sunshine trying to think of something positive to say. 'Next time, mate. Get home safe and kiss those girls for me.'

'Yeah, and you get that record this time,' he replied, then signed off for a quiet beer and restful rain-free slumber.

THE SPEED-CUBED LAW OF DRAG

WE HAD STOPPED by the side of the road somewhere between Kyalite and Moulamein as the late afternoon sun chased dust past us, kicked up by a small convoy of cars pulling up alongside. The driver of the lead car walked over and asked where we were going. Luckily for us he explained that the road we were heading for was closed off. 'She's all shut down, mate, totally flooded.' It seemed surreal that this was happening only an hour away.

We pulled out the map and planned the shortest route to vector around the flooded areas. For the next two hours we skirted the water, staying on the New South Wales side of the border and following the intact banks of the Edward River. The weather stayed warm and still as our convoy gently cruised along quiet back roads through small towns off the grid. The final run into Corowa was a sudden bombardment of insects. The nearby flooding had created a lot more stagnant water than usual so with the sun setting a billion mozzies came out. We had to stop every ten minutes to wipe off several hundred bugs that had smashed into Diego's visor and my face (not one of the joys of a open-faced helmet).

About seven that night we swung into the motel car park, and Diego and I climbed off our bikes, the end of a thirteen-hour ride covering 900 kilometres. Brendan our photographer and Doug our speed data logger were there with beers in their hands; it was a relief to see them, because without their presence we were wasting our time. Everyone smashed down a cold beer then had a shower and it was off to the pub.

Corowa is a quaint town nestled against a bend in the Murray River. Its streets are lined densely with old trees while historic timber-clad buildings lean laconically in one direction or other. The quiet walk to the pub gave me time to think about tomorrow's high-speed run; that eucalypt fragrance so prevalent in the country filled me with optimistic anticipation.

Colin and I were no longer just two guys in a bar planning to go fast on a bike, we had morphed into a team—designers and builders of an outstanding motorcycle and everything that encompasses. But now we had to put it to the test, against the implacable speed-cubed law of drag. If you're male, you will understand the quest for more speed—as pointless an exercise as it may, perhaps, be perceived. All known barriers need to be pushed—whether it's a land-speed record at age 40 or peeing highest up the wall in the school urinal at age eight, it's just the way it is.

In a corner of the pub we talked through the plan, the mood strangely subdued yet charged with excitement. Doug filled us in on what he'd been doing, a massive amount of work. All the various permissions had come in from the airport, council and army. The risk assessment, safety action plan, insurance and airport active radio divert plan were done. We had the runway to ourselves for the hour between 8 and 9 a.m., every box was ticked and the green light was on. 'Sun-up is 6.50 a.m.,' Doug said and went back to his Thai green curry.

Brendan was sitting next to me. 'I've got all my gear ready to go, mate, and the weather forecast is perfect.'

'The main runway is 1887 metres long, 45 metres wide, level asphalt oriented 050/230 degrees magnetic, and has a 200-metre run-off in every direction.' Doug's one of those hyper-accurate guys, it's just his nature, which is great because accuracy is what he does for a living. As I've mentioned he's also a pilot, and flew his own aircraft up to Corowa from his home. There was a pause as he picked up his glass of wine and downed the remains. 'So that's it, it's all up to you now, Paul.' He raised his glass at me and sat back in his chair.

'Don't come off,' Colin added with a grin.

We all turned in early; luckily I was exhausted from the ride and just passed out. Until my alarm clock went off like a howitzer; one by one I could hear the other guys' alarms going off in the thin-walled motel. 'This is it then,' I said to myself.

I stumbled into the shower then out into a glorious sunrise. Colin and Rob were hassling Ed in his room, Brendan was loading his camera gear into his car, Doug was on the phone and Diego was standing at the back of the bike trailer scratching his head.

'Pol, dis bike ees huge,' he said as I wandered over. 'It weel be too heavy for your record, no?'

I shrugged. 'We're going to find out in a couple of hours, mate.'

He held up one of my armoured racing gloves. 'Pol, I am so sorry, but I have lost the other glove.'

'No worries, mate,' I said. I was in a weirdly calm state, but by breakfast time a few minutes later my stomach was in a knot. I wasn't game to eat anything after my last experience with the curry when I nearly gassed myself with my own fart and crashed the bike. So I watched the boys eat their breakfast and tried to clear my mind.

'What's up, champ?' Colin slapped me on the back when we were out in the car park.

I held up the thin leather gloves I'd found to replace the armoured racing ones; I really wished I'd brought along an extra pair.

'Oh,' Colin said and nodded. 'Don't worry about it,

mate. Believe me, if you come off, gloves are the last of your problems. Right, let's get coffee.'

I rode my bike to the airport. The place was perfect, sunny, no wind and a dead-flat, dead-straight runway. We set about marking out the safe braking point with orange traffic cones; Doug prepared his speed data logging equipment and talked to the airport officials and the army parachute display team who were also going through their gear; Brendan set up his camera next to the runway. Diego, Rob, Colin and Ed pushed the BDM-SLS out into the sunshine and checked through all the pre-ride procedures before fuelling her up with Linc Energy's Clean Diesel, while I went up and down the runway on my Harley noting where the slightest undulations were and finding the best line.

Doug waved me over to his spot, set up so he could see everything. 'Okay, there's no air traffic, the army lads are fine, it's 15.8 degrees Celsius, the relative humidity is 79 per cent, there's no wind, the sky is clear, it's not raining, speed data gear is fine. Off you go then.' He smiled, I nodded, pulled down my visor and rode away for a couple of runs on the track. My 1200 Sportster easily eclipsed the required speed and it's by no means a sports bike. Trying to get the BDM-SLS to do the same suddenly looked impossible.

Eight a.m. on the button, I was ready, leathers squeaking as I walked up to the bike; it was just me and her now. Colin, Ed, Diego and Rob were in the V8 Holden Commodore ready to pace me down the runway.

She sat right in the middle behind the 'hold lines', which looks like giant pedestrian crossing, her back wheel right on the edge of the grass. I climbed on. To my right the airport windsock was lifeless, the sun behind me heating up my back. I plugged in the emergency cut-off switch connected to my wrist, hit the fuel pump and cooling system toggles and pressed the engine start switch. The small flat touch-screen monitor which governs the engine management system blinked to life.

'Calm yourself,' I said as I pushed her half tone over on the balance point and toed in the kickstand. Clutch in, there was that nice solid 'thunk' into first gear, gentle revs and I pulled forward to brake and pause in front of the hold lines. It was a weird moment, just like an aircraft would pause before starting a take-off run.

Twisting my head round, I saw the boys were about 5 metres behind me to my far left, Colin revving the car engine and giving me the thumbs-up. There was none of that familiar cooking-oil hungry smoke from Linc's Clean Diesel; there was no smoke at all.

'Ride it like you stole it,' was the last thing Ed said to me.

I flipped down my visor and just hammered it as hard as I could. As she leapt through the gearbox red-lining the gear changes, I held the throttle fully open the whole time and all too soon I was reaching the point where brakes would have been applied at Tailem Bend and it would have been over at 170 kph. But this time I had more blacktop in front of me. In fourth gear

I glanced down, passing 190 kph and still pulling hard as the engine started to shriek under me, vibrations reaching a crescendo as the perimeter of the runway flickered past in a sickening blur. Her revs hit the redline again and another glance down: 200 kph. She was deafening me with noise from the darker reaches of Hades, her vibrations not letting me focus my eyes on the instruments. My peripheral vision liquefied, orange cone, orange cone . . . I had two more seconds on full throttle before I had to brake.

The fear, the very real moment when I reached the braking point and passed it, tore through my mind like acid; my stomach, groin and brain had turned into stone and I could feel my heart pounding on my leathers. Then it went calm, built up to the point where speed, vibration and pressure reached a bizarre balance and for a second we were just flying on air. I was laying over the bike cocooned inside the massive front fairing, wide-eyed and high as a kite, as the end of the runway hurtled towards me at somewhere over 200 kilometres per hour.

Brake! said the voice in my helmet. She dipped down hard, the front forks bottoming out as I squeezed both front and back brakes harder and harder while the end of the runway's hold lines streaked past under my face, which was now doing Edward Munch's 'The Scream' as I desperately tried to stop the bike before we hit the end.

We stopped right on the edge.

My hands slowly unlocked from the bars as smoke drifted up past the front wheel from the completely cooked brakes. The Holden pulled up next to me with three excited faces inside and Colin, who was hyper, leaning out of the open driver's window. 'We couldn't keep up, mate!' he yelled. 'I had my foot buried in the fire wall, and we couldn't keep up.'

'I think my brakes are fucked,' was all I could say. I was shaking, stalling the engine when I tried to turn around.

While Ed and Rob worked on the brakes, Doug checked on the speed data logger. He had clocked the run at 205.48 kph; the record was 210.203 kph. So close.

'Did you get it into fifth gear?' Colin asked as I pulled off my helmet.

'No, mate, I just wound her up to redline in fourth.'

He scratched his chin. 'Try fifth,' he said. 'Although you will lose some revs.'

For the next fifteen minutes we all worked on the bike feverishly, conversations as fast as the tools being passed around. All the bugs had been ironed out for this attempt on the short runway; the frame, the rake and tail on the steering angles, the fuel management system, cooling system, drive and rear wheel sprockets, all fine-tuned around the aim of getting a bike this size down an airport runway as fast as possible and stopping it before the end. This was remarkable when you consider the bike was never designed to be constrained in this way. She was never meant to have massive brakes for stopping hard on the blacktop, but small light brakes to slowly reduce speed on a loose dry salt lake. She could achieve so much on the salt; constraining her was like putting a weight belt on a ballerina.

We went at it again, and at the same point as she shuddered into the calm fourth-gear redline I popped her into fifth, but only for a few seconds, not enough to make a difference. For the next half an hour I went up and down that runway, winding out in fourth, hitting an unfortunate parrot that exploded, popping her into fifth, but we never got close to the speed of that first run. At one stage Doug had to wave me off the runway so a bloke in a light aircraft could land, so we used the time to drain out the Clean Diesel and refuel with bio-diesel. It made no difference at all in the way the bike performed. We tweaked the engine management system; I tried to brake a second later every time, until I was riding off the end of the runway.

We didn't get there in the end, though we got very close. If only we had the chance to see what this bike could do on 16 kilometres of dry salt lake, with the proper DLRA track, officials, Federation Internationale Motorcycle timing gear and everything that makes Speed Week a world-class event. For now, Corowa's 2-kilometre main runway was all we had, and it was over. Frustrating does not begin to describe it. I was accelerating at a rate of 2 kilometres per hour per second; all I needed was another three or four seconds.

IF YOU DON'T BELONG, DON'T BE LONG

THE BOYS WERE happy with our effort; as to whether or not the bike would still be around in a year for a third shot at Speed Week was another question. For me, I had to be patient and resign myself to getting on with normal life without holding on to the hope for yet another year.

We walked Doug over to his plane. I hung around and watched him turn into a speck in the distance, then lay back on the grass next to the runway and enjoyed the spectacle of the army parachute display team hurling themselves out of their aircraft. They morphed from dots in the sky to an amazing coordinated descent, one after the other landing next to me like they were casually stepping off a chairlift. My brother-in-law Dan shares this slightly frightening obsession with throwing himself out of aircraft and off the edge of cliffs; he shows me the footage from his tiny helmet camera and it seriously makes me feel ill.

Diego flopped down next to me followed by Colin and Ed and we all lay there for an hour, idly chatting about the last three years. How close we had come, the excitement and innovation, a bike that was the first of its kind in Australia. Even the Clean Diesel fuel was a first in this country. I was so proud that everyone who worked on this project did it because they wanted to see it work, and work here in Australia, built by Aussies, from the Holden engine to the galah I killed on the runway.

We packed everything into the trailer, car and bikes on autopilot then went back to the motel to clean up, check out and meet up for lunch at the pub. Colin and Ed were heading back to Adelaide where they would try to talk the university into holding on to the bike. Diego and I were heading down to Melbourne and straight on to the 4.30 p.m. ferry to Tassie.

But Colin wasn't quite finished. After we'd done our runs at the airfield he'd poked around the bike for a bit, clipboard in one hand, then back at the motel he'd disappeared, saying he had some calls to make. Halfway through our burgers he casually mentioned, 'I've got an idea.'

We all leant in to hear it.

Colin started talking about British Aerospace, who he worked for when he first arrived in Australia. He'd been on the team that designed a missile system purchased by the Australian Navy and had been sent here to assist with the weapons system being integrated into the maritime theatre of operations. The handover took months as the whole system needed to be tested and the navy personnel had to be trained in its use. This was all done, Colin explained, inside a large secure military live-missile firing range.

Now we were really listening.

Colin paused to drink his beer. 'Well, I've been on the phone and the same army officer who ran the place is still there.' He had a bite of his burger.

'Great, Colin, that's nice. How is he?' I said, suddenly and uncontrollably flooded with hope again.

'The facility has a 5-kilometre dead-straight access road that's used to move the missiles from storage to the firing range.'

'And?' The bastard was torturing me now. He had a bit more burger, another sip of drink.

'And so I asked him if we could run the bike down it. He thought it was a great idea.'

We erupted like a footy team that just learnt that peptides are now allowed in sport, then started firing questions at him all at once.

Colin was grinning madly, but as always remained the voice of reason. 'There's a mile of red tape involved, lads,' he cautioned. 'He needs to put it to the military chain, and we need to be patient. It's not the sort of place you can just ride into.' He was still smiling, though, which gave away his optimism. 'I also spoke to the senior police officer for that area about an hour ago, and he thought it was a great idea, too. He even offered to use his radar gun to register the speed, but it can't go above 200.'

Colin added that the military facility had grown and they now had all kinds of new kit that wasn't available in his time. If we got the go-ahead, we'd also be allowed to play with the army's new toys, courtesy of Colin's mate, including a four-wheel-drive vehicle with what looks like a giant golf ball on the back but is actually a laser-guided missile tracking system. I couldn't wait to tell Doug, he was going to wet his pants.

The five of us dreamt on for another hour, then parted company with the life breathed into us again. Diego and I hit the freeway south towards Melbourne to meet our ferry.

NO WEAPONS ALLOWED

MELBOURNE WAS MORE than 300 kilometres away and it was 11.30 a.m. in Corowa.

'Pol, wat time ees our ferry departing?' Diego was looking at his watch.

'4.30, mate, we better get a wriggle on.'

He looked up. 'A what?'

I fired up my Harley and yelled back at him over the engine noise, 'Never mind, let's go.'

He bounded up to his BMW and performed the Diego Legover: his short frame required a comical run-up and vaulting action as his crotch was much lower than the seat height of the huge bike; he looked like he was humping it. Having said that, once he's mobile he rides like a demon; we exceeded the speed limit constantly. I had to put the hammer down just to keep up with the mad bastard.

We blitzed down the M31 like we just robbed a bank, hitting Melbourne's outskirts which opened into a maniacal blaze of confusing direction choices, usually made at the last millisecond by Diego. He had the GPS telling him in a clipped British accent to turn right in 50 metres. Diego, on the other hand, was convinced he should turn left; although his bike was indicating right, he went left with me in pursuit swearing while weaving through traffic. We went over the Bolte Bridge three times trying to work out if we were going in the right direction and every time poor Diego was hit with a fine; I have a side-mounted licence plate that folds in, so each time we passed a toll I reached back and flipped it in and out of sight.

The *Spirit of Tasmania 1* is a massive vessel that crosses the Bass Strait in a constant to and fro between Melbourne and Devonport, ferrying huge amounts of people, vehicles and truck freight. In fact, the traffic going in and out of Tasmania is so heavy that there's also a second ferry, imaginatively named the *Spirit of Tasmania 2*. Diego and I finally rounded a corner at the end of Waterfront Place and there she was like a floating skyscraper lying on her side in the water.

We pulled up near the entrance to the jetty and lay on a grassy embankment in the sun. One by one other riders appeared; every single bike was a big tourer loaded with gear, sporting huge windscreens and panniers with stickers from all the runs they had been on, engines with more power than my car. They had mountains of kit, thermal jackets, balaclavas, boot liners, neck warmers, insulated gloves—we're talking crazy amounts of gear and luggage. Meanwhile I sat there in a T-shirt and jeans with a run-of-the-mill leather jacket—my gear, or lack thereof, caused some punters to point and laugh. Diego had about the same amount of kit as I did, which was fuck all, though of course his was more stylish.

Diego looked up the weather forecast for Devonport on his phone. 'You know how yesterday the weather was forecast to be fine and with sun and 25 degrees,' he began and I nodded lazily in reply. 'No more, Pol. Now eet ees rain and the showers with high wind gusts and 15 degrees.'

I looked over at the parade of stormtroopers still smiling smugly at us. Now I knew why.

'How you say, we going to freeze our teets off.' Diego laughed at his attempt at Aussie slang and I thought to myself he wouldn't be laughing about it for long.

The boom gate opened and we formed up in a queue waiting to enter the belly of the gargantuan ferry. While the massive line of vehicles waited to board, people got out of cars and stretched their legs, occasionally chatting with other passengers. Here we got our first look at a 'Taswegian', a species of bogan found on the Apple Isle. He emerged from a horrendously battered Kingswood that was parked next to us, wearing pyjama pants and a sauce-stained singlet about 50, overweight; his nose alone suggested large amounts of beer were about to be consumed. He smiled and asked if we were 'goin' tourin'.

Diego froze in complete astonishment before glancing at me.

'Yup,' I replied and smiled.

'First time to Tasmania?' He was openly and unashamedly scratching his balls.

'Yes, we're really looking forward to it.'

He removed his hand from inside his pants and offered it up to shake, I stepped aside and deflected the shake to Diego. 'This is my friend Diego,' I said as the manky ball-sweat-stained-hand was redirected at Diego.

'George,' said the man.

Diego smiled serenely and put his gloves back on—nice move, mate—and shook the offered hand then continued to smile and nod so much he started to look like a stroke victim. I pretended there was a problem with my bike and lay on the ground tinkering with it. Eventually the Taswegian went away and sat on the bonnet of his Kingswood, pulled out his false teeth and started polishing them with his singlet. Diego and I hid behind my bike, consumed with our all-important task of tinkering, while Diego whispered 'Unbelievable' and 'I have never seen anything like eet, Pol'.

We were saved from any more unwanted attention when the crew started boarding the bikes, a process done with predictable efficiency, and before long we had hit our cabins, were showered up and sitting down to a very nice meal in the restaurant. We were both excited at the prospect of five days of riding ahead of us, five days to do whatever the hell we felt like in one of the most beautiful places in the world.

After dinner we moseyed into the bar, which was more like a nightclub it was so packed with happy punters. Even so, Diego's Argentinean mojo reverberated like a compelling bass rhythm and he was soon approached by a stunning young lady who tossed her hair and blushed perfectly. I smiled as I imagined her disappointment when she discovered Diego really is 'just friendly' and stepped out on deck.

As I watched Melbourne get smaller, I pulled a cigar from my backpack and found a quiet spot to sit. I was just starting to lean back ready to enjoy the warm millpond sunset behind the city skyline with my glass of whiskey and a nice fresh Montecristo in my hand when a nasally voice interrupted my daydreaming. 'No weapons allowed, sir.'

I looked up at the middle-aged muppet in a 100 per cent rayon uniform which gave him some minor level of authority. 'What? This little thing?' I held up my tiny pocketknife between my thumb and index finger. 'You don't expect me to bite the end off this, do you?' With my other hand I held up the cigar, which was probably more weapon-like than the 2-inch knife.

'No weapons allowed, sir.' He motioned towards the leather strap of my backpack where a large knife pouch was mounted.

'Oh, that's a flashlight not a knife,' I said.

'Stand up and show me, sir.'

Here we go, I thought. While every punter onboard that ship had been affable and easy-going, I get to discover the one who wasn't, the one who was about to turn into a full-blown ocean-going thundercunt. 'Help yourself.' I slid the backpack across the floor and stayed prone, returning my knife to my pocket and my attention to the fine Melbourne-framed sunset.

He didn't touch the backpack. 'Sir, no weapons allowed.'

I lit the cigar and reached back into my pocket for my knife, got to my feet and looked him in the eye. 'Sir, I understand you're just doing your job.' I handed over the pocketknife. 'Can I get a receipt for that, please?'

Diego walked up to us, having left a trail of broken hearts at the bar. 'Hi guys, wat cho doing?'

The muppet in uniform turned to Diego. 'Do you have any knives on you, sir?'

Diego looked at him then me, pulling his wonderfully whimsical what-the-fuck face.

'He is armed only with a vicious sense of humour and a cock you could hang a wet beach towel on, sir,' I said and put my arm tightly around Diego's shoulder, blowing acrid smoke in our new friend's face.

He left quickly after that, leaving me with a puzzled Diego. 'What ees happening, Pol?'

'Well, the short version is, that security guy now thinks you and I are two gay knife-toting troublemakers.'

Diego looked worried. 'We are not gay, why does he think we are gay?'

I nodded. 'He thinks you are the lady and I am the man.'

At that he went wild, yelling, 'No, no, no, no, eef we were gay, I would be the man gay and you would be the other one.'

'Diego,' I said calmly, turning him to face our reflections in the large glass windows. 'Look at us. You're ridiculously well groomed even by Melbourne standards, you're holding a glass of white wine and wearing a cravat, for fuck's sake.' He gave himself an appraising nod. 'Now look at me—I haven't shaved or changed my undies in two days. I'm the man gay, mate.' He frowned and recoiled a little at the mention of my unclean undies then smiled and waved to the window, having made eye contact with a happy stranger.

I reclaimed my spot in the sun on the deck as well as my almost romantic aspirations for a maritime journey across the great divide, like sailing between the pillars of Hercules with my motorcycle stowed in the belly of the ship. Then, as we stand in a non-gay way on the deck in the morning, egg-and-bacon pie in hand, I thought about how I would feel on seeing Tasmania for the first time.

An hour later I fell into that deep sleep you get on a boat, the last embers of sun glancing off a still sea, the cabin wonderfully quiet and comfortable. At 5.45 a.m. the PA speaker on the ceiling told me we had an hour to be ready to ride off the ferry. My phone beeped; Diego had texted from next door: 'Paul, look out the window, you gay fool.' I got up to the view of Devonport harbour, at least what I could see of it through the driving horizontal rain that lashed everything mercilessly.

An hour later all the stormtroopers rode off the ferry in completely dry comfort. Diego and I made it a few kilometres to a roadhouse and fell through the doors, soaking wet and in need of directions to the nearest motorcycle retail shop. Our wet weather gear was apparently 'water resistant', not 'waterproof' as it had claimed. Diego stood on the verandah, cursing in Spanish while pouring a litre of water from each boot.

STORMTROOPERS

AFTER ENOUGH COFFEE to make me jittery, a hearty breakfast and a lengthy session trying to dry our shirts using the toilet hand-dryer, we tentatively stepped back out into the howling rain and rode to a nearby shop that stocked mountain-climbing equipment, again staggering through the doors like someone just flushed us down the toilet.

'Didn't pack well for the tour, guys,' said the smartarse behind the counter.

'Yeah, yeah, we've been getting laughed at since we got on the ferry.'

He smiled like he'd seen us coming. 'Don't worry, I'll sort you out.' He bounced out from behind his counter and proceeded to flog us $500 worth of wet-weather gear.

Diego was shivering in the corner, his face frozen into a gargoyle smirk. 'May I use your toilet, please?'

'Yeah, mate, help yourself.' In the end our friend was good, he even gave us cups of tea.

Properly tooled up we swaggered out into the street, stormtrooper-clad, warm, dry and ready to man up and take on anything Tassie threw at us. Diego, now 20 pounds heavier and unable to spread his legs as much as he needed to, spent a full five minutes humping his bike in an effort to get on.

We peeled off in the direction of Port Sorell. It was freezing cold; I hadn't ridden in conditions like this since the last time I was in Russia. In fact, the only reminder that we were in Tasmania was the lone wombat we passed by the side of the road, a rather grumpy-looking fellow sitting on a rock with a comedy frosting of snow.

We crossed the Rubicon River as the snow turned into slush and Diego got his ride on. After crossing another river he suddenly turned off towards the national park; there was no traffic on the road so we flogged it. It was wet, but in my mind I justified the speed by telling myself there were no trees, just low scrub, and I'm a stormtrooper now so I'll just bounce if I drop it. Diego finally pulled up when we ran out of blacktop. He killed the engine, flipped up his visor and pointed down the gravel road. 'Let us go and ride on that beeech.' A hundred questions popped into my mind but I just nodded at him, and we were off to ride on the beach while I thought about all the reasons why you shouldn't take a Harley onto the sand.

Having said that, the bike had no issue with it. It was amazing; we blasted up the beach, completely alone. The sand was perfect, like a combination of loose gravel and snow but compacted and solid. My bike is only a Sportster, the lightest of the Harley line-up; this particular model called the '48' has a low, snug riding position, a short rake on the front with huge fat tyres and masses of torque, ideal for riding fast up a beach. I didn't buy this bike to sit in my garage and polish it: I intended to respect it, care for it, but ride the shit out of it. She didn't let me down.

Diego really is a talented rider, if more than a little bonkers. I looked up from my beach-riding daydream, the tune from *Chariots Of Fire* now playing in my head, to see the mad Argy pulling a mono into the surf. Most impressively, he didn't stack it. Wow, I thought, he's equally intent on giving his new German a proper seeing to. What a great place to take your bike; the idea of pulling off the road to ride your bike on the beach would get you shot in Perth.

I was starting to get hungry so we headed for George Town, and even in the appalling weather the riding was sensational; the roads were practically deserted. We skirted the edge of the Narawntapu National Park; it used to be called the Asbestos Range National Park, go figure. Initially I found this extraordinary, but by the end of my first day I realised, that's Tassie—the people are just so relaxed and accommodating that naming a national park after a poisonous material wouldn't bother them in the least while anywhere else it would cause a riot. By the end of the first day I would have gladly pulled over to chat to a random local who just waved me down to the side of the road using a severed head.

George Town offered up a warm fire, awesome hospitality and contented stomachs. Fully fuelled we consulted our map and hit the bikes. We skimmed along empty roads in a state of bliss, stopping again at Bridport, hitting some unsealed road and getting it a bit sideways on the way round, then joining up to the main road, the A3, that plugged us into St Helens for lunch and a brief game of 'Spot the Local'. Then it was back up in another big dogleg after Fingal towards the silly but fun part of the day called 'Jacobs Ladder'. This involved a world-class blat through Ben Lomond National Park; some of it was blacktop and some of it was dirt, all of it was fun. The Ladder is a curious succession of six very steep switchback hairpin climbing turns that slither up the side of the formidably wet and Scottish-looking Ben Lomond. Going off the edge of the ladder was a frightening prospect; any mistake would result in a proper caber toss into a red stain at the bottom, so we took it nice and easy to the top. Sufficiently ready to call it a day, we headed to Launceston for the night having done just over 500 k's since we landed.

Diego had it all worked out. 'I've booked us a bakery,' he said, beaming. I debated whether I should ask for an explanation then decided just to go with it.

Although I have not yet fallen at the altar of Apple and

The Bio Diesel Motorcycle Salt Lake Special—just an engine gearbox and rear swingarm in 2008.

In one piece in late 2009.

And in 2010.

The salt is like riding over crazy paving.

Focused on the endgame.

Speed Week 2013.

Passing the one-mile marker.

Tailem Bend test track—low-flying eagle situation.

Corowa's main runway—no wind, just too short.

Diego and myself—ready for Tassie motorcycle nirvana.

Miles and miles of sideways smiles, and no one else.

Christiaan and Jethro's Beaver sea plane in good company.

The crew of the *Bob Barker*—don't mess with them, especially the small chick at the front.

Diego fast and loose.

That sign.

Bondy, myself and Janelle.

Sydney Harbour shoot for *Australia—Life On The Edge*: Mat is dressed as an officer, I'm the convict next to him, Nathan the cameraman is in the middle, then Russell the director in the stern.

Dirk Hartog Island shoot in WA: Ulrich Krafzik cameraman (left); Eliot Buchan (centre) directs me with flair.

am able to say 'There's an app for that' while someone is talking about hippo mud wrestling, I'm not too proud to admit I was glad Diego had an iPhone. When the sun is going down and you're getting cold and tired on a bike rolling down a random street in a strange town with no information and no plan, that phone is a crackerjack piece of kit.

We pulled up at the rear car park, checked into the bakery (converted into a very nice hotel) and enjoyed another great meal; I fell asleep to the sound of rain on the tin roof and thoughts of home.

Daybreak welcomed us with warm sun, no wind and an urgent need to blat straight down the main freeway that cuts through the centre of Tasmania to Hobart. My friend Christiaan lives there, but he was leaving the next day on a business trip and catching up with him was important because he runs 'Tasmanian Air Adventures'— and has in his possession a beautiful, totally restored 1964 DeHavilland Beaver sea plane.

Christiaan and his full-time pilot Jethro run this operation from the harbour at Sullivans Cove, with Salamanca Market across the street, bang in the middle of all the action Hobart has on the waterfront. Chris spent twenty-plus years as an FA-18 fighter pilot in the RAAF and Jethro flew Tornadoes for Her Majesty's Royal Air Force; between them they have set up a marvellous business. They can take you fishing or camping or sightseeing or drop you off for dinner by a lake or just flat-out scare the piss out of you in a jet fighter that they also play with.

I had not seen Chris in over a year and knew he would have all kinds of good bullshit to swap over a cold one. Diego was equally elated as he had never been in a sea plane before.

We hit the Midland Highway and blasted straight down towards Hobart. I found myself being reminded of Scotland again, then France; Tassie is just a really nice part of the world to go and ride your bike. I guess most of us would have ridden our bikes into the ground as younger men; I'd just ride right through winter with a 'fuck it, it's just water' attitude, but these days I'm driving my car through the colder wetter months and happy to put the heater on if necessary—hell even the heated seat and radio sometimes. Gone are the days when I would compromise comfort or safety to try to look cool.

My bike was superbly comfortable. This new model came with forward controls as standard, while the rear suspension was a bit too rigid so I fitted an aftermarket seat and combined that with an air-hawk cushion; the result was perfect. Harley decided to put a tiny peanut fuel tank on the '48', but even with 8 litres I could get around Tasmania without worrying about running out of fuel. The front end on this bike was wide and had a short wheelbase for a Sportster; the new triple tree now needed to accommodate a 16-inch tyre up front, making the whole thing snug and very low slung. So low that there are 'pavement feelers' fitted to the end of the foot pegs. This is a stud that points down towards the road under your foot pegs, so when you decide to go hard into a corner and lean right over, they hit the deck first and let you know you're about to take the chrome off your pipes. I really couldn't ask for any more from a bike.

One thing that hasn't changed with age is that I still travel light. All I had on me for this trip were the must-haves: a change of clothes and a few, I mean a few, items for personal hygiene like my toothbrush, tyre repair kit with compressed air cylinder, some basic hand tools, cable ties, a 1-litre fuel flask that was more of a mental security blanket than anything else and, of course, our new wet-weather gear.

I slotted in behind Diego and we slipstreamed each other down the Apple Isle, meandering at a comfortable pace, lost in the resonance of engines and wonderful landscapes unfolding over hilltops. Hobart soon came with the coast; we followed Diego's GPS and pulled up at Macquarie Wharf. There in the middle of Kings Pier Marina tied up next to a small jetty was Chris's sea plane.

Diego was doing his excited beam. 'Pol, I can't believe we are going to fly in that plane soon.'

We wandered over to the small office overlooking the marina.

'You must be Paul,' said a guy in neat casual clothes who appeared out of thin air as soon as we walked through the door. 'Jethro Nelson,' he said and shook my hand. He had a warm clean-cut smile and relaxed but organised demeanour, that wonderful combination you get with some ex-military people that puts you immediately at ease just because you can be confident that he knows exactly what he's doing, even in his sleep. He introduced himself to Diego, explained that Chris was at a business meeting and would be back after lunch when he'd give us a safety briefing before we flew off. Jethro was right on top of his game. He gave us a quick tour before parking us in a really nice restaurant next door where he had organised lunch while we waited for Chris to arrive. Lunch was a seafood spectacular that would make Captain Birdseye wet his pants.

'Oi, you in the filthy T-shirt!' There was Chris, looking happier than I'd ever seen him.

We had a quick catch-up then Jethro gave us the rundown on safety and the aircraft, and that was it. The next thing Chris was starting the Beaver's radial engine and in what felt like a few seconds we were airborne and climbing over Hobart, with Mt Wellington as a backdrop, gazing out the window in awe.

Within a very short time we were flying over huge areas of complete wilderness unmarked by any manmade feature. The landscape stretched into the distance flanked by steep snow-capped hills. The Beaver ducked down into a ravine 200 metres deep and tracked along the Gordon River, dropping in with a slight bump and coming to a stop within a remarkably short distance near Sir John Falls. It was a breathtaking ride.

We had a quiet cuppa at the falls, talking about the good old days and just taking in the bush on sensory overload. But it wasn't an idyllic picnic for long.

As we left the river I started to suspect that Chris was having a brain-snap; it pretty much looked like we were taking off directly into a very big wall of vertical rock jutting out of the water. I glanced over my shoulder in time to see Diego's face freeze, only his eyes got bigger. 'This is the good bit,' Chris casually commented over the headsets. I looked at him—he looked like a cab driver stuck in peak hour—then I looked out the windscreen through the spinning prop at rock, everywhere I looked was rock. He pulled hard on the controls and we climbed and banked aggressively but effortlessly, pulling up and away from the ravine wall. I was gripping the side of my seat so hard I cut off the circulation to my fingers.

'Wooooohooo, let us do eet again!' Diego was loving it but thankfully for me we didn't.

On the way back Chris took us all round the city, giving us his rundown on what's what. Touching down in millpond conditions we gently glided back to the pontoon at Kings Pier Marina.

'Beer time, lads,' Jethro announced as we gathered on the jetty.

'Do you drink beer, Diego?' Chris asked.

'Oh yes, I drink the beer very well,' Diego replied.

'Good,' said Chris. 'We have a day off tomorrow, mate.'

THE GREAT ESCAPE

WE PILED INTO a nice trendy-looking bar, found a corner with a couch in it and started drinking.

'Christiaan tells me your father was an RAF navigator.' Jethro was sitting next to me, looking relaxed.

'He was, mate, 11 Squadron for a long time,' I replied.

Jethro's eyebrows raised. 'I was based with 11 Squadron, bit after his time, though.'

'Well, it would have been in the 60s. Dad was in Javelins, I believe.'

He smiled. 'Wonderful aircraft. So is he a bike nut, too?'

I laughed. 'Mad for them, cost him dearly, though.' I went on, 'He got smashed in the officers' mess one day and on a dare tried to ride his bike right through the bar . . .'

Jethro sat forward, his face lit up and to my complete surprise finished the story off. 'He rode up the steps to the entrance, paused on the nice clean red carpet that ran the entire length of the hall, dropped the clutch and sat there pissed while the long red carpet was hurtled out the door under the spinning wheel. He runs out of carpet, the back wheel hits floorboards, flipping his Vincent up into a trophy cabinet, then bursts into flames and the whole fuckin' place nearly goes up—your dad's a legend.'

I was speechless that Jethro knew the story which I had grown up with.

'You know, that bike is mounted on the wall behind the bar now. I used to stand there with a pint looking at it.'

Now I was really stunned; my dad's bike decorating a bar, that I did not know.

'Back in a minute,' Jethro said, glancing at his watch and picking up his phone before going outside.

Christiaan was telling Diego about how the boys amuse themselves on their days off while Diego had that wide-eyed amazed expression on his face. It's hard not be impressed; these guys are motivated on a different level from Diego and I, they have spent decades in a constant state of readiness, relentless training of the mind and body. Then when they leave the service, one that has placed an operational tempo on them that's significantly more demanding than flying a sea plane full of tourists, they find themselves lacking challenges. Building up their business took focus and both men have worked very hard on it; just getting the permission to fly in and out of Kings Pier Marina was a massive achievement. So when they take a few days off, what do you think they do? Chill out and relax?

Fuck, no. They take it in turns to set each other challenges. For example, Jethro will fly Christiaan out into the wilderness, way out, and drop him off with a compass, knife, tent and, in case of emergency, a radio transmitter, then Chris has to make his way back to Hobart in a given time. Next its Jethro's turn, and so on. Of course the challenges also have to get harder and eventually they'll be dropping each other off in their underwear with a can of dairy whip.

These guys are the real deal; they just get on with it, they have nothing to prove to anyone, they have done their duty in peace and in war, more than once. As I write this, both men are flying round the clock, moving victims and trapped holiday-makers away from the catastrophic bushfires that have blazed across Tasmania in the last week. Without any hesitation, they just started flying to the fire front, landing as close as possible to pick up the needy and move them to safety. Bless them both.

'There you go, chap.' Jethro was back and was holding out his phone. On the screen was a photo of my dad's bike, mounted on the wall behind the bar in the RAF officers' mess. 'I just phoned a mate who I knew was a pretty good chance of being in the bar and asked him to take a photo and send it to me,' Jethro explained.

I sent the photo to my dad straightaway, who called me back straightaway. Once we stopped laughing I asked how he was doing, but the cancer was something he didn't want to talk about other than to tell me he was 'fighting'. I went back inside to hear more flying stories, drink more beer, then single malt, and piss ourselves laughing until the sun came up.

When I woke up the next day it was still morning and I was fully dressed on the floor near the bed in our hotel. Diego was on the couch in the lounge room, also fully dressed. Jethro was there as well, but he'd actually removed his shoes and clothes and physically got into a bed and slept like a normal person. He bounded out half an hour later, chirpy and lively, while Diego and I stumbled as far as the wharf across the street looking for coffee.

At the wharf we saw an impressive vessel, big and painted in what I'll call 'waterflage'. I was drawn to it, alone at the end of the pier, no one around, no one on deck, only a big fuck-off set of teeth painted down her bow at the waterline and a Jolly Roger snapping at me through the wind from the top of its line. As we got closer I could see it was not actually a Jolly Roger but rather a skull with a shepherd's crook and trident crossed underneath; she was called the *Bob Barker*.

Rounding the edge of the pier we saw a small trestle table set up next to the gangway with a sign that said

'Free Tours'. A young woman sat there smiling. We looked like a couple of bums in leather jackets, but she sprang from her seat and launched into what turned out to be a really remarkable hour-long visit with the crew of the *Bob Barker*. That flag she sails under is apt; they were patrolling the sea to protect marine life, part of a large and committed organisation called the Sea Shepherd Conservation Society. On this occasion their aim was to harass and track the Japanese whaling fleet. As history will tell you, if you want it done, and it's at sea, you get a pirate to do it.

The *Bob Barker* crew were a focused and determined bunch but we were made to feel very welcome and the tour was an insight into the things that go on out at sea when people don't think you're watching. Of course the Japanese have every right to go whaling, provided of course they do it according to the rules, but they are not. Last year Sea Shepherd saved 500 whales from turning the ocean red with their blood. We all went out on the main bow deck and took a group photo, Diego calling out as he focused his camera, 'Okay, everyone look like hard bastards.' By the time we were back on the pier waving goodbye, I was fired up and mulling over the satisfaction I would get from running down a helpless whaling crew with an aircraft carrier.

That afternoon Diego and I hopped on our bikes and headed south of Hobart down the B68 that tracks the coastline all the way round a small cape then doglegs back up north again. The asphalt gods were good to us that morning, the beautiful green undulating hills revealing picture-postcard town after town with names like Snug, Flowerpot and Woodstock. The road, however, was the opposite of its laidback sleepy surrounds; it was draped like a discarded black necktie over the landscape, serious aggressive riding; as soon as you're out of a blind turn you're already setting up and looking for your exit from the next one. Concentration on the relentless corners should be forcing you to slow down and enjoy the surrounds a bit more. Instead we opted for the riding experience, though we did stop at every town to take a look and almost every town had something interesting to look at as well as the occasional tourist coach to avoid slamming into the back of. It was a weird time of year to tour Tasmania, in between the energetic grey nomad ramblers of summer and the winter walkers.

As we hit the bottom of this little cape, the road offered up wonderful sweeping seaside corners that gave a visual all-clear for any other traffic and an open invitation to lay the bike over, drop a gear and use the whole road to take it as fast as you can. And that's where the local police will nab your arse for speeding, lesson learnt.

Speeding fine neatly folded in my wallet and a friendly wave from the cop who just blew my beer money, we mooched along well under the limit back up the other side of the cape till we hit the A6 at Huonville, turned left and tracked down to Southport. I started thinking about the endless choices for dinner; the food was good, really good here. Progress was stress-free, and we had plenty of time to admire the views.

I was really loving the riding; the road was completely empty, the weather was warming up with the sun bathing more colour into the landscape. Tasmania has some of the most unspoilt and dramatic scenery anywhere in Australia. It's also tidy; I wasn't scanning the pavement for dog turds or praying I don't step on a needle at the beach.

Coming around another meandering corner through deeply green rolling fields pepper-potted with tin-roofed, thick-timbered barns, any random one of which I would gladly convert into a holiday home in my private helmet screening of 'Paul's Barn Conversion Grand Design', we hit the edge of a huge forest and the whole thing starts to look like Switzerland, but without the associated smug smell of melting chocolate and money. With the greying aged barns floating on a sea of green waving grass, backlit by forest and hills, I was suddenly insane with the need to just ride into the fields, up the ever increasing hills . . . being chased by the Germans atop badly disguised Triumph motorcycles. My imagination went wild. *Yes, oh yes* . . . there was a break in the fence line and a clear dirt road that stopped after 10 metres, unleashing an open grand green Valhalla of a field for my complete and total encapsulation of the full *Great Escape* moment.

I smoked the rear tyre on the brake drifting sideways then flung the bike into the turn-off, Diego slamming on his brakes as he passed. It was a total split-second spur-of-the-moment thing; I was too far gone to stop, totally caught up in the setting, completely alone. All I could hear was the Harley's roar as I stood up on the pegs and started rocking the bike on its springs; my rear wheel spun towards the apex of a silky smooth crest, straight over the top of Julie Andrews, the chase music now playing full pelt in my lid. I glanced over my shoulder at the imaginary German riders closing fast, the one on my right now racking the charging handle on his MP-40 machine gun looking to draw a bead over the front of his sidecar. The crest approached, I was now fully convinced the universe would provide a perfectly made, rubber, 10-foot high barbed wire fence propped up with genuine imitation rubber tree posts for me to jump over.

But, no, instead there was an angry farmer who looked like he was in the middle of gender reassignment surgery sitting on his tractor yelling at me to get the fuck off his property. I returned to the road where Diego was parked with a knowing look on his face. 'Okay, you have eet out of your seestem now?' he asked.

'When I get home I'm going to get a 650 Twin Metisse Desert Sled.'

He grinned at me then roared off towards South-port. By five in the afternoon it was starting to get cold, my mind had wandered back to food, and that was all I could think about until we got to the end of the road in Southport where there was absolutely nothing to eat. We turned around and bolted back towards Hobart's colonial sandstone smorgasbord of fine-dining choices and our warm well-appointed hotel, where hot showers and tomorrow's Salamanca Market awaited us.

DEFECATION MACHINE

WE ROSE EARLY to another sunny Hobart morning, went out into the market as vendors were setting up their stalls, ate a massive breakfast, drank too much coffee and wandered about like an old jittery married couple for an hour. Then we snapped out of it and rode off north this time.

From the city we took the Brooker Highway through the suburbs and on to what I thought was going to be another circular lap to the right, past Sorell and down to Port Arthur, then back to Hobart. But our day of riding was cut short when Diego turned off the highway and steered us into the car park of Mona, the Museum of Old and New Art. It was just mild curiosity that drew Diego there, but within the first hour in Mona I knew we would be spending most of the day in this remarkable place.

We had no idea what to expect from the museum so the entrance alone was enough to captivate our curiosity. The beginning of the journey started with a nice modern building where we were greeted at the door, then handed an 'O' device which was just like an iPhone with white earphones. This was our guide through the gallery. Then we descended into an ink-black bizarrely deep and expansive labyrinth of huge halls cut into the stone. It wasn't laid out like any other museum I've set foot in. Like a cross between a Bond villain's lair and a really trendy nuclear bunker full of iconic tributes to modern design that melts into the art that in turn reveals itself in a quiet private way. The place was full of people wandering about in silence with earphone cables dangling through the darkness, like zombies that just found the back door to Steve Jobs' basement. But because it was so dark and quiet it felt like they weren't there, just the overwhelming sensation of vast space within the blackness. It was slightly foreboding but strangely it felt safe and peaceful down there. A fascinating exploration through an impressive collection.

Well, I was impressed and feeling at peace right up to the point where art imitates life in a bad way, in the form of a piece located within a separate room that was attached to a huge open gallery. It was simply entitled 'A Defecation Machine'. I stood in the open doorway, looking at the brief synopsis on my 'O' device under the heading

'Artwank', expecting to see a transformer dropping what looked like King Kong's finger into a huge stainless steel potty. But, no, the first thing that hit me was the revolting smell. It was completely unexpected but those clever people at Mona have a series of high pressure air vents running all the way around the entrance that keep the smell out of the main hall. So you wander into the room all happy and bewildered only to retch the second your head clears the entrance. Dangling neatly from the roof were five manmade glass stomachs (which were labelled 'Gastro-intestinal Machines'). I didn't stay in there long enough to find out what happens next; suffice to say I'd absorbed enough artwank for one day.

The time passed as if through the looking glass, ending at a rather nice bar cleaved through solid stone, with single malts and cool languid echoing surrounds; it was like drinking and falling asleep in a cathedral and we emerged blinking and slightly euphoric like two middle-aged clubbers. The light was fading as we pulled away from Mona; it's a place I will definitely return to one day.

Back at our hotel in Hobart after another top-notch meal and more whiskey, we were slightly tipsy and about to call it a night when we noticed that the nice people from the hotel had left us a complimentary bottle of wine. Following the revelation that this was indeed free to swill, we were shabby again the next morning— shabby as in a cross between shit and crappy. We paid the bill, checked out, and Diego pulled on his helmet and sat on his bike in quiet pain while I had a long think about whether or not I was going to vomit, my own alcoholic breath swirling in my helmet making me gulp for fresh air.

We retraced our steps, this time turning off towards the airport and over the first of four bridges. My head cleared as we crossed the last bridge and went south again. Sorell provided much-needed coffee and friendly locals who welcomed us into their cafe with its pressed tablecloths and faster broadband than Telstra manages in central Sydney.

The sun was out again, slowly warming my back, as Diego led us along the Arthur Highway towards two isolated peninsulas; the first, Forester, is connected to the Apple Isle by the thinnest thread of land then bulges out into the Tasman Sea, narrowing again to an equally thin thread at Eaglehawk Neck before ballooning into the Tasman Peninsula. We passed through Dunalley heading for Port Arthur but I'm not going to harp on about the disaster that befell the area in the past; instead I'll just say that the people are what make this place special, they add to the natural beauty like the icing on a hippy's cake, in a knit your own muesli, life is like that, now get on with it, kind of way.

The first peninsula is also special because it's a natural 'buffer zone' for the Tasman Peninsula, the only area free of disease for the Tasmanian devil. For the past thirteen or so years, these remarkable and tough little creatures have been plagued with a form of cancer that is threatening to wipe out this unique species. No one knows what caused it, but let's hope they find a cure soon. There's a conservation park just off the highway where you can see the devils in real life, another species fighting to stay around a little longer.

After circling round through Port Arthur we cruised back the way we came to Sorell for more tea and cake then rode north, tracking up the eastern seaboard. Off to our right across the iron cold sea was another amazing green-on-blue peninsula, Freycinet National Park, with the granite peaks of the Hazards providing an imposing backdrop. We pulled up in Swansea and sat back to enjoy a late lunch of local wine and amazing fresh seafood, before ambling further up the coast, riding with no real plan or sense of urgency, watching the landscape transcend through a myriad of golden shades and tones as the sun came to rest moment-arily on the horizon, flickered and disappeared into the night.

We stopped at St Helens, found a place to stay and after hot showers, hit-the-spot pub food and good banter with the locals, we fell into our rooms with no alarm clocks set and slept like logs.

Diego banged on my door early, the sun was just up. 'Pol, eet's time to ride, my friend.' He thumped on the door again.

'Okay, okay, I'm up,' I yelled at him from under the covers.

'I weel be waiting out the front, okay?' To which I said nothing. 'Fifteen minutes we go.'

Last night over a counter meal at the bar—after I'd explained to the locals that we're not a gay couple, but if we were I'd be the man gay because I don't eat quiche, I eat egg-and-bacon pie, and I'm not wearing a cravat—Diego and I looked at the map and decided to ride directly across Tasmania from right to left, so that was the plan for the day: head out from St Helens straight across to Queenstown with a dip down to Melton Mowbray in the middle.

I had time for a quick shower and to get my gear on and I was out the front in fifteen, then had a few more minutes to warm up my bike while Diego did his legover and mounted his. We fuelled up and blazed our way south, criss-crossing the landscape as the sun slowly warmed the earth. As usual there was no one else on the road, and we took it in turns to lead through k after k of increasingly faster bends, cutting our way through the patchwork of lime green and banana yellow fields to hit our lefthander at the Midland Highway and start the dogleg down to Melton Mowbray.

At Oatlands we had fresh bread rolls, homemade jam, and tea made with love and brewed in a pot that was older than the town. Friendly locals stopped to chat as they entered the cafe, ringing the bell on the door. I looked out the window and on cue a boy riding an old scooter raced down the sidewalk with a stick rattling in his hand as he dragged it across the fence palings while being chased by a slightly dopey-looking labrador. We were in a 1950s midwestern American movie and I was waiting for the guy at the counter to say, 'What'll it be, mister?'

I'd been out of the loop for almost a week. I didn't know what was going in the media, politics, the world. I had no idea how either of my businesses were going, I hadn't spoken to my family for three days. Compelled by the immediacy of this sudden realisation, I spent the next hour on the phone. My wife was fine, the kids were fine, although my son had discovered spitting a few days ago and had since been mercilessly gobbing on anyone who strayed into his own personal target-rich environment. Just that morning, Clare said, he'd already gobbed on the postman, our neighbours and their dog.

Jason filled me in on business, as did Gregg. Everything was just peachy, except for my father; he was maintaining his stiff British upper lip while all along I knew that his reassurances over the phone were rubbish, I could hear it in his voice, between the breaths and smothered pain. I put my phone back into my saddlebag and sat on the kerb, trying to think of something positive to say to my father the next time we talked.

Diego came out into the sun and fired me up. 'Come, Pol, let us ride into the mountains.' He grinned at a random passerby, swaggered over to his bike then stopped and pointed at the road in front of him where two thick black burnt-rubber tyre marks snaked up the road courtesy of some idiotic petrol head. 'Look, Pol, ees bogan tracks,' Diego said, proudly showing off his command of the vernacular. Then he pushed his bike forward onto the road looking like a midget walking a rhino, humped his leg over it and rode off down the street.

Half an hour later as we wafted along, the sun disappeared like a giant light switch in the sky had just been flicked off; we both raised our lids skyward to see dark brooding clouds collide. The temperature slowly dropped as we started to climb higher above sea level towards the formidable Cradle Mountain. Into the depths of Tasmania's wilderness it became clear that it was getting much colder. We pulled over just as the blacktop ran out, giving way to a wide dirt road, to pull on more layers. I unfurled my hand from the bars and realised my fingers were snap-frozen. Diego was excited, but of course he had a heated seat and grips, Günter gently massaging his bottom over the rough unsealed road that was about to shake my kidneys loose and make my bowel feel like I just had a 5-pound concrete enema.

Riding a remote dirt road at speed for the first time is always a bit hectic, but this one turned out to be a joy. Initially the corrugations were a b-b-b-b-b-it jittery so I stopped to let some air out of the Harley's giant tyres and then ride faster, fast enough to plane over the top, epic fun. Rooster tails flung dirt into the sky as we throttled on, round hugely long sweeping corners, so long that I was accelerating the rear slide on full lock until I thought the circle must be complete, but then another one started. We slid and roared into an ancient forest, shattering the silence and tearing up the dust. My bike stayed as slick and slippery as Diego in a dinner jacket and I was having a ball. We were still climbing as the woods became thick with heatless layers of light, mist and cloud evolving above the treeline, then descending past us into the folds of the valleys, filling up like a Spielberg effect below me.

We rounded another climbing lefthander side by side, then on the apex of the bend we heard it first, a residual rumble over the top of our engines, bouncing and reverberating off the forest at us. Then—*fucking hell*—two massive lumber trucks, also running side by side, rounded the corner straight at us. With only seconds to react we just fluked it and made the right choices. Diego and I came together in the middle and the two trucks separated and ran the outside. Everyone entered the massive dust cloud together. The trucks made a hole, Diego and I touched elbows, gritted teeth and disappeared into it. As soon as we passed the trucks and were out the other side, we both stopped and sat there for a few moments, completely blind in a red cloud until the dust started to settle and we could actually see one another. I was about to say something but Diego just gave a mumbled shout from inside his helmet and bolted off, leaving me in another cloud. I love that crazy bastard.

PAVEMENT FEELERS

I FOUND DIEGO by the side of the road making a snowman. We had turned off the dirt and were now heading towards Queenstown. He spun around when he heard me. 'Snow,' he said, like he'd just invented the wheel, and turned back to his pile. I never expected that we would be going from a balmy 26 by the east coast to just above freezing and snowmen by lunchtime, but that's Tasmania for you.

Turned out my mate had never seen snow before, so we had an impromptu session involving all the snow stuff. If this were a film it would be the bit where you're looking at the 'snow montage', with us throwing snow-balls, putting a helmet on the snowman, laying down on the roadside and making snow angels, etc., with a nice background sound bite of chirpy and sickening pop. Instead, it started raining, hard, the snow instantly turned to slush, then cold water, the music stopped and we were now standing in the pelting rain, soaking wet and getting mildly hypothermic miles from anywhere.

Out came the wet-weather gear. As we attempted to dry off a bit under the trees and pull on our waterproof suits, I suddenly realised there was something different, and it's not something you get on a road trip that often. Apart from the occasional clap of thunder in the distance and the rain itself, and our bikes occasionally popping and pinging as their hot steel cooled in the cascade, it was quiet—total silence. The only two vehicles we had seen on the road that day were the trucks that nearly turned us into hood ornaments.

Diego had noticed a sign just up the road and wandered over to take a closer look. 'Pol, how big do the kangaroos get here?' he asked, pointing at the sign.

I looked at the sign and it, combined with Diego's quizzical face distended in real concern, made me laugh. The sign was definitely not to scale and I could see how it could be confusing for a foreigner. It appeared to be saying three things to the happy motorist: first, you should be doing 65 kph; secondly, under the heading 'Wildlife', there was a visual warning of giant albino kangaroos as big as your car; and lastly that they will from 'dusk to dawn' leap out of the bush and perform a snatch-lift on your front bumper. All it needed was a Monty Python foot smashing down on you as you read the sign.

We rode on. I was getting worried about my fuel; my tank was on reserve and good for less than 20 kilometres. Diego was infallible when I started honking on with my fuel concerns. 'Do not worry, my friend, there weel be a station for petrol just up the road,' and with a big gesticulation towards the west he belted off deeper into the woods. My bike coughed after five minutes, then hacked like a fish gulping in air but looking for water. I pulled over straightaway, rummaged through my saddle-bags, found my fuel flask and poured in the one litre, hopped on and started praying for a roadhouse. I had a length of hose to drain fuel from Diego's ample tank if I needed to, but that was a last option. Just as I was about to run dry again I saw the pot of gold at the end of the petroleum rainbow, the Derwent Bridge roadhouse.

We fuelled up, pushed our bikes round the side, went in and ordered a big lunch then sat in the corner to wait while slowly drying out and heating up. The place was deserted; no one else came through, there were no other cars or bikes around. After lunch we wandered outside with big hot mugs of tea and lay on benches watching the sun slowly blink through the windblown clouds, not a sound, just the wind in the trees, our bellies full of homecooked pasta and properly brewed tea. Both of us promptly fell asleep.

I woke with a start, almost rolling off the bench. Diego was snoring, his empty mug still sitting on his chest slowly going up and down. I checked my watch; two hours had gone by, we were losing daylight fast. I gave him a shake and we both lumbered round the corner towards the bikes, only to discover two large salty-looking possums trying to hotwire my Harley. They had already dumped the contents of one of my saddlebags on the ground and had a good look through my shaving kit, managing to also cover each other in shaving cream. Sprung, they ran off into the trees and sat there above us, chewing on my muesli bars and smelling of lemon.

The sun came through for a look as the road shook the last of the slush off its gravel shoulders and began to dry out. Daylight slowly turned orange as the sun dipped behind the hills, setting off the landscape in rich deep purple and green. As the light faded, so captivating was the view luxuriously opening up in front of us that I didn't see the possum. (You know this story isn't going to end well.) We'd just rounded a corner at the top of a forested hill, a long dry straight forcing Diego to down-shift and gun his bike well past the limit. I followed suit and tucked in over the tank. The possum had, evidently, waited for Diego to fly past then decided to run into the middle of the road and plant a face-first kamikaze headbutt straight into my bike; there were perhaps two seconds between me seeing and hitting it. The bike took a terrible jolt, I veered off to the right with a high-speed wobble and a little tank-slapping then straightened up and continued on. It was pointless stopping; Diego had streaked ahead and would have no idea that I nearly came off, and the possum, well, let's just say at least its death was instant.

So I caught up with him, then we crossed the Lake Burby bridge and stopped next to an ominous-looking concrete building in the middle of nowhere called 'The Linda Valley Cafe'. Diego was chatting to several other riders who all stopped talking and started laughing when I pulled up. 'What did you hit, mate?' one of them called out.

I looked down; the poor possum had basically exploded when hit by my Harley doing about 140 kilo-metres per hour. It was like someone had just thrown a bucket of red paint over me, and when I took off my lid it was to the smell of slow-cooked possum baked on engine and pipes; there were only a few chunks left clinging to the underside.

Joined by Diego's new friends, we rode on in a small convoy down to Queenstown. The road was a dream, opening up into a deep valley, with a steep twisting descent of corners that switch back all the way down. The other lads waved as they continued on and we pulled up for a beer and a motel bed.

Our last full day in Tasmania was going to be our best— I didn't know it yet but I was about to have a truly great ride. We started with another wonderful sunny morning, the hills steeped in mist as the day rose. We stood on the motel's porch and pondered our route back to Devonport and the evening ferry to Melbourne. We mapped out a big ride that took us south from Queenstown to Strahan, then back up to Zeehan, Rosebery, up the A10 to Wynyard on the coast, then left all the way to the bizarrely named 'Dismal Swamp Forest Walk'—there are loads of forest walks to do in Tasmania but we knew we had to do that one. From there it was a run straight to the ferry, about 600 k's and eight hours in total.

The ride out of Queenstown to Strahan was just perfect; the sun was shining, the road empty as usual. Huge ferns grew from the high banks of the shoulder straight up with the forest and bowed over, totally enclosing the road; our headlights gleamed into the green tube, like riding through a rainforest tunnel. Breakfast in the small township of Strahan and on towards the north and the coast. The whole day played out in a series of dreamily idyllic places and moments. We started seeing other riders, and Diego was constantly enthralled in the history of wherever we were, asking questions of anyone and everyone who would stop to chat, but our journey was slowly coming to an end.

We rode on in complete bliss, just ambling through the countryside, then we hit the hills again. Diego was in front as the road began to skirt up the side of Hellyer Gorge and down into the almost tropical valley. He was in the zone, faster into the corners, proper supertight hairpin, frame-scraping corners, the ones where the sign tells you to take it at fifteen. It was steep and winding, the inside banks of the road began to camber up in our favour, higher and higher. So Diego began to use them, hitting the apex on the edge of the bitumen at 60 and laying his bike right over, popping up a gear for a few seconds then downshift and high on the camber into the next one.

We started overtaking each other, we could see it was clear ahead so we used the whole road. My head was clutter-free, I was having such a good time, every corner had my pipes hitting the road, pavement feelers long since worn down and I didn't give a shit anymore; I was actually trying to lay the bike down and couldn't. The bank of the road was too enticing, something to push against and tease through the corners: it was a lock-in at Disneyland. I rolled the throttle harder and earlier in the turns, only remembering I was riding a Harley when the ground fell away under me and it was only the centrifugal force keeping the tyres on the road, then the suspension bottomed out on the back wheel under the compressive force and I was sling-shotted out of the turn and into another one.

We reached the end, both of us pulled up, paused, silently nodded back in the direction we had just come, and turned around and rode it again the other way, then doubled back and did it again. It was epic fun, on a perfect sunny day in Tasmania.

Our run to the coast was easy and relaxed. We saw the ocean at Wynyard and turned left, riding together all the way to the western seaboard at Arthur River, with just enough time for a cuppa and another stopover for the very pleasant Dismal Swamp. Then it was a blast straight to Devonport with more and more riders popping out of the woodwork to join up in a convoy that ended in the queue to board the ferry.

As the sun started to set we all mooched about talking bikes and where we had been; every single rider, from retirees in their 60s to young lads on slick sports bikes, had the same smile on their face. It was a scene that could play out almost anywhere at any point in the history of motorcycle riding; like surfers standing beachside scanning the waves, so too bike riders bounce the experience off each other in a timeless way, their hands weaving to demonstrate as they describe a corner just taken, in the same way the surfer narrates a nice bottom turn.

JACOBSON AIRLINES

THE FERRY NAZI and my pocketknife were nowhere to be found, so Diego and I finished our meal in one of the restaurants on the *Spirit of Tasmania 1* and settled in for the night. The ferry was very comfortable and catered for the entertainment of its passengers, including a free cinema, where Diego opted to go while I lumbered off to bed.

It was nice to wake up with the sun shining through my window on a big boat, Melbourne slowly getting closer as I grabbed a shower and packed my gear. Diego was already loading up his bike in the vast steel car park below decks when I got there. We rode into the morning traffic, heading directly north for my mate Clayton's place.

An hour later we rolled into his property. Large and sprawling, Clay's home is wonderfully peaceful, and as usual he was straight into stories and music. We had a great meal and sat on his huge porch admiring the unspoilt rolling green view. Diego spotted a boomerang hanging on the wall and the next thing I know Clay had him hurling it all over a paddock while his horses pranced about looking nervous. Next was the compulsory bullwhip-cracking session; Diego managed to crack the back of his head and I removed a slice off the top of my right ear.

Then we hit the off-road toys. Clay has a flat-out scary thing called a Polaris RZR, an off-road buggy that merged with a transformer then drank too much Red Bull and went mad. Clay told us to go and get our helmets on and come back in clothes we didn't mind getting 'a bit mucky'.

Clay's toy is the size of a small car, seats four adults in comfort but goes like a dirt bike. It's got everything you need to go from zero to 100 in ten seconds over rough uneven bush, plus instant selection between 4WD and 2WD—you just push a button on the dash, then get some air. When I say air I mean Clay was broadsiding dirt 20 feet into the air behind us, cresting a rise in the middle of a paddock and hitting his jump, no warning. There was just enough time during the flight for Diego and I to turn and look at each other, screaming, then look back at where we were going and panic. Fun does not begin to describe it.

An hour later we were both fucked with matching internal bleeding and bruised kidneys, and 200 pounds of mud liberally sprayed from head to toe. There was mud inside my helmet, there was mud inside my eyelids.

The next day, feeling a little sore, I waved Diego off. The crazy bastard decided he was not done yet and rode back to Perth from Melbourne. We had been fortunate enough to do some epic rides on incredible roads and have the kind of adventures that I'll rant about all my life. I know one day when I'm old and kicking about period-ically peeing myself I'll be telling my grandkids about the time I went to Tasmania with a mad Argy called Diego.

That night Clay and I explored the finer points of brandy and opened a nice cognac. He has a limit-less ability to stimulate the mind: he writes so well he actually makes a living from his talent; he's a musician, too, and a bloody film director, amalgamating all this with a natural skill that makes it look easy. Sometimes I can't keep up with Clay's brain box when he shoots off in several different directions simultaneously. I struggle with the simple stuff; my own alchemy of writing is, as you know by now, just storytelling. But Clay bends and moulds the narrative into sculpture beyond the word, he sees things in four dimensions and, much to his disdain these days, 3D as well. 'Fuck 3D,' he scowled from inside his Tardis-like collection of movies.

'Let's watch this,' he said, holding up Alan Parker's *Angel Heart*.

'Nahh,' I said and he returned to the shelves.

'How about this? The first *Alien* movie.'

'Nahh.'

Clay gave me a look. 'Okay, you choose then.'

But there was too much to choose from. 'Let's watch telly,' I optimistically suggested.

Clay laughed. 'That comes down to three things: the time of day, the channel and the state of the nation.' He glanced at his watch. 'The news is on, but that's it. After that it's a depressing slide into mass commercial unimaginative mainstream structured reality slop.'

I grinned, knowing full well that he'd just shot a TV show and several ads of the mainstream slop kind in the last few months.

The phone rang; it was an Indian telemarketing call centre and in a sudden flurry of activity Clay hit the speakerphone button, raced into his office where he has an impressive mountain of editing and sound-mixing equipment, and instantly through the surround sound there was the background noise of people, movement and intermittent radio chatter.

'Identify yourself, please,' Clay said in a voice that was perfectly authoritative and slightly intimidating.

There was a brief pause. The call-centre chick sitting in Mumbai was probably a bit baffled but she tested the water anyway. 'Hello, my name is Jody and I am calling you today from Sydney. How are you this evening?'

Clay hit another button and there was a burst of shouting and a siren. 'Well, Jody,' he said, 'my name is Detective Sergeant Addams. Listen carefully: there's a crime scene at this address, so I will need to know your full name and residential details in Sydney, and the reason for your call.'

And she was gone faster than our super in a government bond.

'Well played, mate,' I said, suitably impressed.

He grinned. 'I've got a few different scenarios, in different languages.'

The phone rang again. 'Good evening, The Savoy Grill, Adam speaking,' Clay's voice went up five octaves.

We settled in for the night, watching the sun set on his balcony. My bike was getting freighted back to Perth and tomorrow I would be on a flight home, then a week later another one to San Francisco, then Houston for the annual Offshore Technology Conference, the biggest conglomeration of all things oil and gas on the planet, and four days of total mayhem.

Perth blasted me with heat and paint-stripping sun as I walked out of the airport and headed straight to my office. The rest of the day was meetings followed by a bizarre phone call from my agent. *National Geographic* was about to shoot a television series on the history of Australia called *Australia—Life On The Edge* and they wanted me to go and do a screen test as one of the presenters. I had been approached for a screen test once before with *Top Gear Australia*, and in retrospect I'm lucky

I was 'too British' or 'not Aussie enough' as the show was axed after going through two different versions with two different networks. But I agreed to this as it sounded exciting; it was different, the budget was huge, they had seven one-hour episodes to shoot involving helicopters, a two-man submarine, diving, rappelling, all kinds of vessels, shipwrecks, desert and bush adventures—shit, I didn't need any more convincing.

Two days later I was sitting in a survival suit strapped via a four-point harness with a rebreather on inside a helicopter fuselage mock-up dangling over a large pool about to do HUET (helicopter underwater escape training). Five very nice people were there, the director, cameraman, soundman, the runner and the makeup lady. They wanted to see if I could remember my lines while doing something challenging.

Could I deliver a nice piece to camera about how important safety and training is in the modern world of oil and gas exploration? Could I keep talking and maintain eye contact with the camera while the helicopter landed, water poured in and the whole thing started to sink and invert until it was completely upside down and submerged? Could I keep talking while the water rushed over my head, then unlock the door and open it, undo my harness, make my escape, inflate my life vest and break the surface correctly orientated towards the camera, spit some water out of my mouth and continue my monologue to the camera like nothing has happened? Could I hold the audience's attention, project my voice over the chopper rotor sound effects, gesticulate enough but not too much and not look like I just got flushed down the toilet?

No, I could not. I forgot my lines, inhaled water, choked, popped up on the wrong side of the chopper with half a pint of snot hanging out of my nose and delivered my lines to the microphone boom not the camera. But they were patient, explaining that the large thing which looked like 'Chewbacca's penis on a stick' was in fact the sound recording device, and eventually I got it right. They shook my hand and said, 'We'll be in touch,' and with that I went home to pack for the United States of America.

ENGLISH CARS. SCOTTISH WHISKEY. AMERICAN SERVICE

I FLEW EMIRATES, and that's it. No horror stories, no dramas, no loss of bowel control or missed connections, no screaming kids or fearful moments, no crazy people, nothing. It was a business–class bullshit-free experience and I loved every minute of it.

I arrived in San Francisco mid–afternoon. I was there to visit two old friends; they sent me instructions to catch a bus, and there it was right opposite the entrance to the airport. That was so easy it was just weird. I got on the bus and the driver launched out of his seat in shock because I was carrying my bag.

'Sir, please, let me stow that for you,' he said and bolted off to put my grip bag in the luggage hold, then leapt back on the bus and showed me my seat, asked me if I was familiar with San Francisco, gave me a tourist brochure, smiled and told me we would be off in five minutes and it would take 45 minutes for us to reach my stop at Larkspur Landing, all ending with another big smile, not fake, just a big 'Welcome to the US'.

Holy shit. I'm used to the lack-lustre half-arse attitude you get about 50 per cent of the time in Australia, especially in Perth. Where I come from 'Just fuck off' is visible in the thought-bubble hovering over the heads of everyone who deals with the public, from the dude in my local video store and the woman who brought me the wrong coffee, to the guy who came to do the termite treatment on our house last month; he was about to start drilling holes all over my place, until I reminded him that our house sits on cement pillars. There's the woman who tried to sell my wife a mobile phone, the guy who was supposed to be selling me a leather sofa last week, and so on.

But there is also a definitive gap, as abrupt and apparent as the class system in Britain in the 1800s. Luxury items, for example. You can go and buy a Jaguar and there will be service with a fully vetted and approved smile, you will get tea and cake, they will come and pick up the car from your home and service it, clean it and bring it back, leaving another Jaguar for you to drive if you need to go out and receive shitty service.

My car told me it was having a problem with an engine fluid level the other day, so I just drove to the dealer, arriving unannounced to tea and cake and a nice chat, and would I like to read today's paper or do I need a lift back to my office? The good people at Roadbend returned the car to me two hours later, having fixed the problem, and they cleaned it, I mean properly cleaned it inside and out. And here's the good part: no bill. I was flummoxed by this because in the usual scheme of things, you check in for the service and check out with a bill the size of Somalia's national debt, but, no, Mr Tony Percival said, 'Not at all, Mr Carter, it's our pleasure.' Why can't it all be like this? He knows I'm now in love with his business and will purchase another car soon, not just for the tea and cake but for the service. Try that shit with your phone provider or the people you just purchased all your white goods from and they'll piss themselves laughing at you.

I knew our levels of everyday customer service were lacking, but it's been some years since I was last in the US and I had forgotten how service-driven they are over there. Wages obviously are a big part of that, but this dude was a bus driver. Do you tip a bus driver? Minimum wage is very low so people rely on a 'gratuity' when you pay the bill and as a result you do get the most phenomenal service. In Australia the attitude is completely different; your employee will arrive on time feeling like you should be grateful because they actually turned up in the first place. I know this because I have eighteen employees and it took two years to find the right ones, none of whom are Australian, which is sad and even embarrassing to say, but true and probably not all that surprising.

I arrived at Larkspur Landing, hopped off the bus, gave the driver a tip as he handed me my bag and sat on a park bench overlooking a clean, almost empty car park next to the terminal for the ferry that perpetually transports people to and from the city across the impressive bay. I heard the car before I saw it. Sally and Simon Dominguez's battleship-sized 1979 Special Edition 'Bill Blass' Lincoln Continental. Even though they weren't deliberately driving like maniacs, the massive 21-foot-long two-door coupe's tyres squealed like dying rabbits as they hurtled rounded the corner and pulled up in the car park grinning like a couple of outpatients. The Lincoln was all blue leather, the hula-hoop-sized steering wheel sat in front of the hilarious instrument cluster; all chrome and long with a Cartier clock at the end, it looked like my grandmother's silver service. Simon sat in the back sprawled out like a pungent bum in a leather dumpster. The car was bigger than the flat I grew up in. The best part about seeing old friends after a few years is picking up right where you left off. We went straight to their local for, according to Simon, the best margaritas in town.

The Silver Peso was busy. Simon introduced me to the barman, telling him I needed a margarita.

'Welcome, Aussie,' the barman said, shaking my hand. 'Would you like an eight-dollar or ten-dollar margarita?'

I went for the ten-dollar option and by the time I'd finished shaking a few other hands the barman passed me a bucket of margarita and, once I'd finished it, I was wrecked. Sally was on fire and making me laugh so hard I was crying. She's golden, firing at full pace and volume from the moment she opens her eyes every day. She complements Simon's laconic, almost lucid lethargy; if he was any more laidback you'd think he'd suffered a stroke. But that's just Simon, and he's not at all how he appears. He's supremely fit, smart and very level-headed, just lucky to be able to switch it all off and relax. Two hours later I stumbled through their front door, managed not to vomit on their children and passed out on the couch to Simon telling me something about their house being in the liquefaction zone should there be another earthquake.

San Francisco in the bright glorious Californian sun is a wonderful city. I jumped on the practically empty mid-morning ferry and sat on the main deck with a bloody mary as we motored through the massive bay, devoid of the famous fog, past Alcatraz, with the Golden Gate Bridge providing an impressive backdrop. It's a huge sprawling place where steep hills descend through a myriad of eclectic but perfectly preened multimillion-dollar homes that tumble down the hill and up in price as you get closer to the water. It's the kind of place where I could live if circumstances allowed, but nothing is impossible. Sally and Simon are mates from Sydney. They went to San Francisco on a holiday years ago, then one day they just said, 'Fuck it, we're moving.' Now almost six years later they have a successful business, two very happy children and a really nice life in this place.

But there is more to the city than nice bridges and expensive hillside real estate; I was lucky to have Simon and Sally to introduce me to all kinds of different people. San Francisco is the birthplace of Levi's jeans and the martini, and it's been the mecca for every bright young mind who turned over a billion on a dot-com since the late 1990s. It's trendy high fashion that's affordable, it's the epicentre of the hippy and the earthquake. I rejoiced in all she had to offer by spending up big, mincing out into the late afternoon in a nice off-the-rack Tom Ford two-piece navy blue suit, British cutaway collar, Alden handmade polished black brogues and silk-knit black tie; they even threw in a glass of brandy and petal-soft matching socks.

Retail therapy, as they say, was working for me. I felt wonderful, having just dumped the clothes I left the house in that morning in a bin outside the boutique like the remains of my former self. I was going to enjoy a bar-hop stroll, I was going to have a martini, shaken, and not by the earthquake. I turned from the bin, adjusting my cufflinks, and ran straight into a polite but shabby hippy.

'Hey, hi, can I have your clothes, brother? I see you're tossing that bag.' He looked like a cross between a cocker spaniel and Elmo, right down to the badly dilated sad eyes.

'Sure, mate.' I reached back into the bin and handed him the big paper bag with the boutique logo and my former skin.

'Thank you, friend,' said Elmo.

'Not at all.'

I started to walk away when he called out, 'You're British, right?' I turned without stopping and nodded as he yelled at me, 'Good for you, man, enjoy the city.'

With pleasure, I thought, and that was how it turned out. I didn't know it at the time but my walk was about to lead me through Castro, the biggest gay and lesbian neighbourhood in the US, and as you would imagine it's a hub of sartorial refinement, very polite, stylish bars and more shopping, with more great service.

As the sun set I found myself faced with a choice of scotch whiskey laid out on the bar in front of me. Miles Davis mixing nicely with conversation in the background, I surveyed the stash being liberated from wooden cabinets . . . and, *bang*, there she was, almost empty, a Speyside malt from the Macallan distillery, year of our lord 1967. When that single malt was being bottled in Scotland, this city was giving birth to the hippy revolution that saw more than 100 000 people join together and kick off the start of modern cultural and political change, and then they all shagged each other silly and produced my generation.

I paid the man and took my time. There was a nice spot in the bar where I could survey the street life, spark up a small cigar without offending anyone and enjoy the end of a very old bottle. No scorched throat here, just a revelation of rich flavours unfurled over my tongue beneath the alcohol's harder notes. Like a favourite song or the smell of a delicious meal coming out of the oven at home; I shut my eyes just for a moment and let my memory unfold at the same rate. All the way back to Woodside Avenue, Grantown-on-Spey, Dad, playing alone in Free Church Wood behind the house, and the first time I smelled this combination of barley, water, yeast, peat and oak; simple elements, yes, but in the hands of the artisans who do the business at Macallan, they make so much more than the sum of their parts, right here, right now, 45 years later. It's not a bottle of whiskey; it's a time machine with an international adaptor on it. Like some of my friends it doesn't mix well with others but fuck, get to know it and you have something you'll enjoy for life.

'Thank you.' I smiled and tipped the barman.

'Don't mention it, Mr Carter. Have a good night, sir.' He got the door for me. If only I could make this a week-long Groundhog Day.

I met up with Sally and Simon at the restaurant they'd chosen for dinner. They are the perfect bohemian couple, at peace with each other and the world. Their friends were equally funny and just mad enough to make me feel like we used to, before we had responsibilities and businesses and kids and shit. Our night went into morning, I did the required cable car ride, danced badly to Jimmy Buffet and managed to dip my new tie in my clam chowder.

The next thing I knew I was getting off the plane at George Bush Intercontinental Airport and looking at my friend Gregg Cooper in Houston, Texas. We hopped into another Lincoln, but this time a modern 'Town Car'.

Gregg looked relaxed as he pulled on the column shift, popping the giant car into drive and gliding out of the car park and onto a huge highway. 'So how was California?' he asked.

I told him all about San Francisco, Tom Ford suits and tab collared shirts, the cable car, the whiskey, especially the whiskey. We talked about gun-related crime and my expectation—based on the fact that the US accounts for 5 per cent of the world's population and 50 per cent of the world's guns—to be mugged or shot in a drive-by while I was strolling alone in evening.

'Well, just about everyone here is armed,' Gregg explained, 'but you don't get that much crime because of it. I mean, break into someone's home or try and jack a car in this city and you'll get shot at.'

I smiled a nervous smile and wondered how many hand guns were in the gloveboxes around us.

'Road Coke,' Gregg said and handed me a can of beer.

We cruised to our hotel in the city and settled in. Tomorrow was day one of oil and gas madness that would see 100 000 people under one roof for four days.

H'TOWN

THE OFFSHORE TECHNOLOGY Conference (OTC) is a melting pot of just about every side of oil and gas, a madhouse four-day event involving people and firms from more than 100 different countries. I knew it was big, but I had no idea how big until I got to the Reliant Center; it's a little overwhelming, the car park alone is big enough to land a space shuttle in. Houston's clear sky radiated the heat of the blacktop up my trouser legs and down the back of my shirt.

We entered through the main doors, wheezing, and stood in the air-conditioning as thousands of people milled about. It made me tired just looking at it through the noise and gleaming corporate polish as I wandered randomly like a kid lost in the toy department, surrounded by so much new technology, innovation and flat-out remarkable shiny stuff, realising well and truly that my old job on an offshore drilling rig was superseded by a machine years ago. I found myself feeling nostalgic at one point when I rounded the side of a huge display stand with an entire land rig sitting in the middle of it and stumbled into a series of good old-fashioned rig tongs. So it wasn't all fly-by-wire, integrated hydraulics, cyber chair, go faster all the time—some things are still done the old way—but having said that everything seemed to be getting bigger, more high-vis, fireproof and lighter.

My job was to visit the stand of Jet-Lube, a firm who I do business with in Australia through Gregg. They asked me to sign my books and to generally mingle, chat, talk about the oil patch, and of course the advancements Jet-Lube have made in grease technology. I had some public-speaking gigs lined up as well.

'You ready for this, champ?' said Gregg when we got to the Jet-Lube stand. It was massive. They had posters with me on them and 'Booth Bunnies'—basically two scantily clad eighteen-year-olds with dazzling teeth and wonderful gravity-defying body parts who slid across the stand and into the crowd in Jet-Lube's black and orange colours.

I was completely unprepared for the rush when the book signing started. I'm used to the occasional book signing after a writers' festival or something like that, but this shit was out of control; this was rig hands and scientists elbow to elbow, mothers and students, full–on flat-out for the next two hours. My writing hand was useless after the first 200 copies had gone; the last 50 looked like my son Sid had been doodling on the covers.

I beat a retreat to the Red Wing stand and hid among the coveralls, but I was in America, where standing idle in someone's stand at their biggest trade show will have a fully clued-up bunny-assisted company representative front and centre, eyeball to eyeball and ready to answer your questions within 0.01 of a second.

'Good morning, sir.'

I turned and smiled, still holding onto the trouser leg of a pair of their coveralls. 'Great kit, Red Wing,' I said, trying not to look at the bunny's breasts in the background.

'You bet,' said Red Wing man. 'You've worn Red Wing before?'

I was about to tell him I spent twenty years in them when another Red Wing man bounded over. He looked like the bunny keeper. 'Hey, are you Paul Carter?'

What the fuck's going on, I thought, then tentatively answered, 'Yes.'

And that was it. He disappeared and came back with about 50 people who wanted to meet me and we spent the next hour swapping phone numbers and taking hundreds of photos. I backed out of the Red Wing stand with armfuls of gear and boots and baseball caps and cup holders, but no bunny, promising to return the next day to meet the Red Wing man in charge.

'Beer time.' Gregg appeared behind me, thank god, because I was quite lost. 'I can't believe how fuckin' popular you are.'

'Thanks.'

He laughed. 'Don't these people know you're a dickhead?' He hustled me through a side door and into the searing Houston daylight.

'I guess not, Gregg.'

He looked at all the Red Wing stuff and pulled a raised eyebrow at me. 'Well, I say milk that puppy till it's dead, buddy.'

We had lunch in a restaurant with a barbecue in the courtyard that was so big it had its own dual-axle trailer to move it around. After eating half a cow and drinking my body weight in beer, I wandered into a boot shop and just stood there for ten minutes looking at thousands of pairs of cowboy boots. Bang, there was a dude in a fabulous pearl-snap shirt.

'Good afternoon, sir.' He was good, and within minutes I was swaggering out of a change room looking like Roy Rogers.

I know it's a cliché but everything is bigger in Texas; my hotel room was huge, the car was huge, the hooters in Hooters were huge. Houston, however, presents it all to you in a wonderfully polite way.

I was on Gregg Cooper's all-you-can-eat tour of Houston that ended at Montrose. Westheimer Road was alive with people, music spilled out of shopfronts, bookstores and neon-lit tattoo parlours and flooded the street.

We walloped through the door and into a bar called Poison Girl, part-owned by a mate of Gregg's. The place was exactly where one should hang out with Gregg. It was a long thin bar with a high roof cross-braced with dark thick exposed wooden beams, bright pink walls, and big ceiling fans whipping a rotor wash of old wood and beer past an eclectic bunch of characters propped up at the bar, nursing everything from a banana daiquiri to a pint of cider. We waded in past the locals and started Gregg Cooper's one-on-one school of American whiskey appreciation.

His mates turned up, then it was 'Randy and Jeff and Garry and Garry's mate Bill and a random guy who walked in looking for directions and Gregg's' magical mystery tour of sour mash whiskey that will, and I mean it will, make you go blind. Poison Girl has more than 200 varieties to choose from, and Randy was quietly talking to the barman who disappeared and came back with 'something special'. I can't remember what it was because I went blind and had a nap for a bit, then woke up in front of another steak the size of Tasmania.

'He's okay!' shouted one of the boys. I had lost some time here. It was now dark and everyone was lit up in pink neon.

I laughed that night, Gregg's friends were just plain fun. We stood at the entrance to the hotel waving them off. Randy drives a 600-horsepower Camaro that sounds like an air-raid siren eating a tiger; I could still hear him leaving as we rode up to our floor in the lift.

Now that I'd been fully vetted into the H'Town bourbon appreciation club, Gregg announced that tomorrow's festivities would include a Mexican breakfast, a visit to the Jet-Lube factory, and my choice of any one of the eighteen museums in Houston.

For most people from my part of the world, the name 'Houston' conjures up thoughts of drilling rigs and oil, not the sheer volume and choice of culture, art and theatre and the brainwashingly good food; and as for the locals, well, if you're a polite person any random Houstonian will fall over themselves to help. This place is also the country's centre for healthcare and medical research, and it has a large population of students as well. I went to sleep that night thinking about the space centre, perhaps a visit to NASA, but as is my want, everything just ends at Hooters.

OTC day two, post Mexican breakfast, double the punters turned up looking to get a signed book and at least one of the bunny's phone numbers. I talked and talked until my voice started to go, then beat another retreat, this time to Gregg's place where we had some lunch and decided to go shooting for the afternoon. His place is not too far from the airport, so I could grab a shower and make my late afternoon flight to Dubai and then home.

Now unlike Australia, the United States, as we all know, has a different policy on firearms. In Texas, to go out with a gun, shooting as a sport or pastime, is as normal an activity as fishing or footy or taking the dog for a walk. So we arrived at Gregg's local gun-range-slash-store-slash-wonderland and, of course, it was huge and empty because everyone was at the OTC. The lady behind the counter was extremely nice, asking straight-away if I was visiting from overseas and was elated to hear that I had come all the way from Australia; she gave me a tour of her facility that included a shop with a small arms section that started with handguns. A glass counter top stretched some 50 feet down the length of the back wall containing just pistols, and from there it escalated to shotguns, rifles and all the hundreds of products that spin off an arms market like no other.

Gregg, being used to all this, elected to leave me there with his 70-year-old M1911A1 pistol, John Browning's pivotal handgun design that stayed with the US armed forces for the next 74 years. He could see I was going to be happy and just told me to give him a call when I needed picking up. That was me taken care of for the rest of the day. I purchased several hundred 45 rounds and went to the outdoor range. Other shooters soon turned up with all kinds of weapons.

'Mornin',' said one guy and smiled.

I smiled back.

'Nice day,' said another.

'Nice old piece,' commented a big man with an army-issue haircut.

Within five minutes they had me in a shooting merry-go-round that lasted the rest of the afternoon and would have gone on into the evening had Gregg not turned up to tell me I was in imminent danger of missing my flight.

There was a rushed shaking of hands and thankyous as he bundled me into his Lincoln and took off towards the airport.

'Sorry, mate.' I coughed up all the usual excuses but he just smiled knowingly.

'I've got your bag in the back, I just didn't want you to miss your flight, buddy.'

We were about to get on the freeway when he slammed on the brakes and started swearing. Then he looked at me.

'What?' I didn't like this.

'You're not going anywhere, man.' He looked at his watch.

'Why not? What the fuck are you talk about?'

'You just took a four-hour bath in nitrates.'

This was not enough to make the question mark scrolling down my face go away so Gregg explained as he threw a U-turn and sped off in the opposite direction to the airport. 'I can't believe I didn't think of it—you're covered in gunshot residue, Pauli. You'll have ten cops and five dogs on top of you if you try to check in for a flight.'

The penny dropped. 'Oh fuck, what now?'

'Shopping.' He pulled into a Wal-Mart car park and hustled me into menswear and up to another fully vetted, fully prepared and fully willing middle-aged woman to whom he explained our predicament to, and she was off like a middle-aged rocket. 'Come with me, young man.'

I followed while she fired questions over her shoulder at me about sizes and grabbed shoes, shirts, pants, the works. I stripped in the change room as fast as possible.

'Have you enjoyed your visit to Texas?' she said while handing me clothing over the top of the change room door.

'Oh yes, it's been wonderful.' Fully dressed I swung open the door, my gear lying on the floor in a pile behind me.

'Don't worry about that, come on with me,' she said and led me to a bathroom at the back of the store.

It took just fifteen minutes to get me fully kitted up in Levi's jeans, Haines T-shirt, a pair of Converse, with a place to wash my face and hands thrown in, and get back in the car headed for the airport with time to make my flight, the bill $78.

Gregg dropped me off laughing and went home to clean his gun. I walked into the Emirates check-in section at Houston Intercontinental to no queue: my first reaction to this was the usual 'Is it the right day, the right time?' followed by the hurried checking of one's itinerary and scanning of the airline staff while trying to figure out which was most approachable. Turned out it was the right day and the right time, just no one else showed up.

So I checked in and strolled through the empty customs and immigration area where they had a big clear tube you stand in that sniffs you for the two most prevalent things that make the world go round, drugs and things that go bang. It beeps, and lights up, then there's a 300-pound policeman leading you into a little room where two more big Texas policemen fill opposite corners, smile and ask you how you're doing.

'Fine, thanks,' I said and smiled like a man who thinks he's about to get fisted in a cavity search that puts the 3D into *Journey to the Center of the Earth*. I had visions of an inflatable neck brace being the last of US purchases on this trip, except I wouldn't be using it for my neck.

'Mr Carter,' Cop One was studying my passport, 'we've detected trace elements of explosive material on your person.' He paused for effect and folded his arms making his bicep flex until it was the same size as my head and gave me a hard direct stare; you know the one, where he's picturing himself taking my head off with a shovel.

Cop Two spoke up from behind, putting my head on a swivel. 'Can you tell us why, sir?'

He was pulling on a black surgical glove now, and I was thinking, Black, why is it black?

I realised my explanation was blurted out so quickly I started to go back in time.

'Mr Carter, relax, have a seat.' Cop Three gestured towards the empty chair in the only corner not filled with a uniform, so I sat down and explained myself to them, and for me this involved starting at the beginning. I suppose about half an hour went by without me taking a breath. Other officers came in to listen as I covered everything: why I was in the US in the first place, Americans I'd worked with, Afghanistan, reasons why I should not have brought up Afghanistan, oil, drinking, eating, OTC, more oil, Hooters, Poison Girl, American customer service, Australian gun laws, oil again, books, free books, free signed books, Wal-Mart, the shooting range.

'I just bought everything I'm wearing,' I blabbered, smiling and pulling out the Wal-Mart receipt. 'I scrubbed down and dumped all my kit, even my belt.'

The big Texan cops were all sitting down now, listening and nodding, because my stories tend to go on a bit and go off on a tangent, especially if I think I'm in imminent danger of getting fisted. 'Right, thank you, Mr Carter, that'll be all we need,' said Cop One. 'Have a nice flight, sir.'

I nervously stood up. 'I can go?'

'Yup, we found very small traces of nitrates on your wristwatch, nothing to worry about.'

The watch was the only thing I didn't wash. I couldn't resist and paused halfway out the door. 'So what if I hadn't stopped at Wal-Mart on the way here?'

Cop One stopped smiling and gave me the shovel look. 'You'd be missing your flight.'

I nodded in that fisted way and got out of there.

BONDED

JANELLE VAN DE VELDE has an excellent phone manner, speaking like a woman who is so organised she already knows what you're going to say before you say it. She is meticulous and in possession of an excellent sense of humour. So when you eventually meet her and come unravelled during your business meeting, she is delicate and able to restore your fragile male ego so you don't walk away from said meeting looking like a total idiot. You are, however, now acutely aware that you just got your arse handed to you by a charming woman, who was better dressed than you, taller than you (excluding heels) and more experienced than you in business.

I'm relatively new at this, being in business, being a businessman, the art of negotiation, of war. Learning that there are no friends in business. Judging who is who and where they fit in based on what they want. The information kings and the misinformation muppets.

Watching Janelle deal with her business, in her capacity as Linc Energy's President of Shared Services, I realised how well she plays the game. Even more interesting was being invited to be part of Mr Peter Bond's first jet flight across Australia using Linc Energy's synthetic Jet A-1 fuel. I had lots of experience with Linc's Clean Diesel fuel and found the process of producing that remarkable, to say the least.

As I mentioned earlier, Peter Bond is an interesting chap. A self-made man, his company now sets the pace in Australia for pushing the boundaries of exploring the future of affordable fuel. The fact that he went from an idea to producing fully vetted and internationally approved jet fuel that's cheaper to produce and cheaper to purchase than the current fuel is just amazing; when you take into account the fact that he did it in five years, it's staggering.

So when Peter is walking through a cow paddock, he knows there is coal below his feet at a thousand feet, he knows he can turn that coal into gas, then turn that gas into a clean fuel, then turn that fuel into jet fuel, and do it safely, with a minimal environmental impact, and make it all happen so it's cost-effective in today's dollars. Then just to prove it works, he sticks his new jet fuel in his own aircraft and flies it from Perth to Adelaide to Melbourne to Canberra to Sydney to Brisbane to Chinchilla.

At the end of the day he's managed to produce fuel at a cheaper price that burns more efficiently and produces fewer emissions than conventional fuels. He's come a long way in his 50 years, from a trainee metallurgist down at BHP Steel's coke ovens in the Illawarra, in New South Wales, to a rich guy in his own jet flying on his own fuel to his own island. I say, 'Well done' and 'May I please have another glass of that Macallan?' and 'Can I please go and sit in the cockpit?'.

He is also fascinating to watch in business, except he operates on a different level than the one I'm just beginning to understand, the one where I get to see him metaphysically shove his entire arm up some corporate oil executive's bottom and work him like a puppet.

Frankly, I'm just happy sitting in the corner nursing a single malt that's older than me and eating rinky-dinky handmade canapés offered up by a supermodel and made by a genuine candidate for the master-chef master-classy school of cocktail nibbles. Nibbles made from things you only see on telly and sometimes pass in an overpriced gourmet deli in a suburb you're only in because you got lost. Food that is picked up between your thumb and forefinger with an extended pinkie and balanced on a napkin. I'm hungry and standing behind the scenes as best I can, hiding behind a very tall man in a tailored grey Prince of Wales check suit and polished dark brown brogues and the impeccable Janelle van de Velde.

Mr Bond is in the throes of delivering a rousing address to the packed room overlooking his jet. The media is there, the TV networks are there, politicians are there—Canberra is BP-slick tonight and all I can think about is my empty stomach. It's rumbling loud enough to make the occasional person look around; I'm drooling like Pavlov's dog over the food that's being quietly laid out on tables. As covertly and surreptitiously as possible, I stop being hypnotised by the amazing spread right next to me and just give in, faking a slight cough and stuffing five canapés in my mouth at once.

'Special thanks to Paul Carter for joining us today—perhaps a few words from Paul.'

Fuuucckk! The inner scream fills my head. Lights search the room and I'm instantly lit up, lenses find their target and pull focus, my cheeks, now distended with canapé and whiskey, flush bright red, catching all the light in the room. I'm busted like an impatient greedy thief, I'm guilty as Kelly, Ned Kelly that is. All I need now is the bucket, not to wear over my head but to spit the contents of my mouth into.

'Nicely done on the talking with your mouth full to the country's news media earlier,' Mr Bond's full-time pilot Kane says to me later.

'It takes great skill,' I reply, smiling. He smiles back and hands me another scotch. 'It's a gift, really. I don't like to talk about it.'

Kane and I stand there surrounded by deeply serious political, financial and heavily business-orientated conversation. We know we're out of our depth and unable to jump in on any level, so we revert back to looking like we're also engaged in big-boy I'm-a-player man talk.

'So how many canapés do you think I could get in my mouth?' I ask him, nodding at another table festooned in more gold-clad delicacies.

'Well,' he pauses in reflection as we glance around the room, 'you give me a kiss, and I'll tell you.'

I look over the rim of my glasses at him like we've just struck the biggest covert deal in political, financial and business history. 'Dickhead.'

Kane nods then gives his best nonchalant smile to a middle-aged woman in a sheer black silk dress who glides past then he announces that he's off to talk to her about her vagina and leaves me there in no man's land.

One thousand two hundred canapés later I fall into my tennis-court-sized bed in my hotel suite. Mr Bond's jet awaits the next morning.

Problem is, I'm starting to get used to this life. I sit at the back of the jet next to Mrs Bond. She's lovely and blonde but not in a blonde way; the fact that she was finishing the crossword in the *Australian* in the same amount of time it takes me to read the front page should have alerted me this.

'So you're a writer?' she politely asked me, and I nod, cutting straight to 'What's it like living on your own island?' I picture the other Bond's nemesis in a villainous lair hidden inside a volcano jutting out of the middle. 'I mean, how do you do the shopping?' Possibly the silliest question one could ask a woman like Mrs Bond and immediately I feel stupid. But Mrs Bond, of course, has her feet firmly planted on the ground. She is so down to earth it's like chatting to my sister, and this, of course, just made the experience even more accept-able, easy, even expected—we fly, we schmoose, we canapé. And why? Because we can, because Mr Bond's got affordable, eco-friendly jet fuel, he's the George Clooney of jet fuel, and me, well, I was grateful for the free Clean Diesel he gave me last year to run the bike on. I certainly didn't expect to get an invitation to fly the high life in his jet in the process. But when you're Mr Bond you get to do that.

I am transported home with all the pampering and civility imaginable. I feel like the Queen Mother by the time I open the car door and step onto my suburban driveway. My neighbour Nick is watering his garden as Mr Bond's limo tools off down the street.

'What the fuck have you been doing?' he asks, hose in one hand, bottle of beer in the other.

'Flying all over the country on a new environmentally friendly aviation fuel that's going to revolutionise the jet fuel industry and pave the way for innovative Aussies to show the rest of the world how it's done.'

'Fuck off, Pauli,' he says and shakes my hand.

The next day I sat in my office trying to remember if the whole jet caper had actually happened; it was so surreal

it seemed far away. The week stretched past slowly, punctuated by canapé flashbacks, until my old friend Erwin
phoned me up to tell me he was off whatever god-awful
drilling operation he'd been on and was now home and
keen to jump on his bike.

As requested I arrived on my bike in his front yard
7 a.m. sharp on a sunny Saturday morning, brandish-
ing the thousand-dollar carbon-fibre helmet I'd decided
to purchase for Speed Week (if indeed Speed Week ever
actually happened), and there he was, sitting on his porch
drinking coffee, as solid and reliable as gravity. Erwin is
a constant in my life; he remains as steadfast now as he
did when I was twenty, and he still looks the same to me,
only time has greyed the edges.

'Nice lid,' he said as I bounded up the steps to his
porch. 'Pity.' He gulped his coffee.

'What is?' I asked, sitting down.

'The dog's pissing in it.'

'What?'

I spun around in time to see Boston shaking off the
last few drops on the rim of my upturned no-longer-
smells-like-brand-new carbon-fibre helmet. That dog
lets go like a racehorse. I spent an hour washing it out
while Erwin got his bike out of storage mode. He kept
laughing whenever the image of Boston popped into his
head. 'Sorry, mate,' he said repeatedly. 'How's your lid?'

I had finished handwashing the liner and scrubbing
out the inside, but it didn't really matter what or how
much I tried. I slipped my head inside its superlight

carbony Darth Vader slick cottonwool internals, and for a second everything was fine, like shoving your head into an Aston Martin's glovebox, then finding a sodden nappy in the corner.

The day only got better. When we finally got Erwin's bike started and it looked like we would actually go for a ride, it pelted down. So I decided to take his bike up the road for a wet spin, and promptly dropped it while turning into his driveway and broke the big toe on my right foot. Erwin was gracious about it; the bike, a three-year-old Harley VRod, was barely scratched but my foot was a mess.

Off to hospital, home with pain meds and the diagnosis that I would need foot surgery to fix the problem. I had to wait a few days before my appointment with the orthopaedic surgeon and, as things are in life, this was when I got the phone call from *National Geographic* telling me I'd been cast and the contract was on its way over. It arrived with a breakdown of the content of the series; it all looked full-on, with lots and lots of things involving a fully functioning and reliable big toe.

So then I went to see the surgeon and he got to the bit where they talk about recovery from the operation. 'You're going to be incapacitated and without normal mobility for three months, Paul, so if there's any reason why you can't do this, we can postpone the procedure until later.' He chewed on the end of his pen and searched my face for any type of reaction.

'Postpone for how long?'

'Well, not more than six months, at the most.'

I explained my situation after which he gave me more drugs and showed me how to tape up my foot. He also gave me a special shoe insert that stopped my toe from moving too much and that was it.

I didn't tell a soul at *National Geographic* about my toe, so a week later, script not yet memorised, toe throbbing in period-accurate boots, I emerged from a wardrobe trailer, dressed circa 1788 convict, into the middle of a packed Circular Quay at Sydney Harbour, completely unprepared.

1788—THE YEAR OF MIGRATING DANGEROUSLY

RUSSELL VINES WAS the director. A big man, big and hairy in a nice way, he had lots and lots of experience filming hard, tough stuff on the fly. His last television directorial effort won awards and was the first series to cover on any level the stages of selection into the Special Air Service Regiment; *SAS—The Search For Warriors* would have been a difficult shoot for him and his crew. And of course all the guys on the crew had lots of experience; we were roughly around the same age too. Meanwhile I had bucketloads of dialogue to learn, lots of factoids to inject at appropriate moments, and the whole lot left my head like David Copperfield's jet the moment the trailer door cracked sunlight onto my woolly and extremely itchy wardrobe ensemble.

'Lovely, you look suitably hot and uncomfortable,' Russell said, glancing up from his gear as he set up his shot.

This would be the first image in the *National Geographic* series *Australia—Life On The Edge*, seven one-hour episodes covering pivotal moments in our country's history and starting with the big one, the arrival of the First Fleet into Sydney Cove. There were four presenters involved in the series, three of them wonderfully qualified, experienced around cameras and good-looking—Mat McLachlan (historian), Giovanna Fasanelli (marine scientist and submarine pilot), Andrew Bales (geologist)—and me (I don't have a special talent, eating canapés perhaps, although I used to paint when I was an alcoholic). I realised I was the odd one out as soon as I started holding my gut in and couldn't remember factoid number one, my name.

Russell was supremely patient with me, as was the other director, Eliot Buchan; they knew exactly what to say and how to put me at ease. That's hard as I'm easily distracted, especially when the first shoot is in the middle of Circular Quay during the morning peak-hour rush. They needed to fence off random people from walking into the shot, Russell and Eliot had this sixth sense, they would break from conversation, snap their gaze into the middle distance, look at a crew member and say, 'Jeff, at your two o'clock,' then straight back to the conversation. Jeff bolts off into the throng; he's a guy on the crew whose job is to deal with 'squeezers'. A squeezer is anyone in authority who will walk up to the crew regardless of what they're doing and start demanding to see their varied forms of permission to film there, their insurance or safety or parking or lighting permit, or permit to be bald, or the official onsite filming authority that states that the filming can only be for fifteen minutes, in a southwesterly direction not to be panned up by more than 20 degrees, and everyone's got to be dressed in blue. Shit like that, shit that had been signed off by the squeezer's boss's boss weeks earlier with a follow-up call, email, carrier pigeon sent that morning as a reminder. Squeezer control is a full-time gig.

I got nervous as Russell and Eliot began walking me through the first shot and I started to realise that lots of money was involved, that eight people on the crew and dozens of others representing harbour safety, the marine police and the council were all there watching, and the knock-on effect this had on all the ferries, tour boats and public transport that come and go from the epicentre of the harbour and were now on hold while we got this shot. In fact, the whole day was going to be spent collecting what would equate to somewhere around six to eight minutes of screen time on the final cut.

'Right, so we're going to be tracking from that boat there,' Russell said, pointing at a special camera boat rig, then pointing out that he had a camera on top of the Harbour Bridge, another one on a special stick on the jetty, and one on a fucking helicopter as well.

'Okay, then,' my voice had turned into a nervous squeak.

Mat to my right was confidently nodding while the sound recordist Jason North was wiring me up and saw the shit I was packing. 'Don't worry, champ, you'll piss this in,' Mat said. I faked a smile and got nauseous.

In this scene, Mat and I, respectively dressed as 18th-century English ship's officer and convict, had to row an equally period-accurate boat into the harbour, stopping as close as possible to the actual point where the real First Fleet rowed ashore. This involved getting the shot from multiple angles while we faultlessly rowed like the wind, avoiding the world's second-largest cruise ship moored at the overseas passenger terminal. We were sitting next to each other with an oar each, rowing towards number 6 quay but not facing the direction we were going. 'I'm fucked already.' I looked at Mat who wasn't even sweating yet.

'Mate, stick to the dialogue,' he said, laughing. 'Whatever the fuck happens, just make sure we don't row too close to that cruise liner, okay?'

Russell's camera boat started to pull closer and he gave us some direction via a radio transmitter under our seat. 'Guys, just make sure you don't get too close to the liner.' We nodded and I glanced over my shoulder to check; there was noise, lots of people cheering, and we looked up to see hundreds of silver-haired pensioners waving at us from several different decks way up in the air above us.

'Stand by, camera rolling,' said the voice under my seat, and then we rowed, big, steady, we-could-do-this-shit-for-a-living rowing. 'That's great, guys, keep going, Paul look over to your right at the Opera House, Mat at the Harbour Bridge, yes, perfect, we're pulling back and coming around towards the front, just keep going, yes, oh, the light is perfect there, not too close to the . . . turn left, left, the other left, fuckin' port, to port—'

Bang! the hard metallic clang of wood into world's second-largest cruise liner caused the pensioners to go into hyperdrive. Then we heard, '*Get that thing away from my ship!*' and Mat and I nearly capsized in shock as the booming voice of God came down over our heads and reverberated across Sydney Harbour.

'And that's the world's second-largest penis speaking into the world's second-largest loudspeaker,' Mat said and grinned at me.

Woop woop woop! We jumped again and spun around to see the water police beside us. 'Gents, throw us your line there and we'll give you a quick tow over to where you're supposed to be,' one of the water rats said.

I threw them our line and soon we were back in the right place and ready to do our dialogue. This involved me pulling out a painstakingly replicated copy of an early map from the time of the First Fleet, making sure we didn't drift back for a second time into the second-largest penis. It worked, somehow, I have no idea how, and my brain regurgitated all my dialogue with no mistakes.

'Got it, that's perfect.' Russell was happy.

They got the big sweeping visuals, the close-ups, the whole introduction to the series. After we climbed out of the boat and waited for the next location move, another chap appeared in front of Mat and I holding collapsible chairs with built-in shade and proceeded to ask us about food. 'Hi, guys, I'm Bill, the runner. Coffee, sandwich, Danish, smoke, bacon-and-egg roll, newspaper, phone, whadya need?' Mat and I exchanged blank looks. In front of us the crew were packing up what looked like half a tonne of gear into huge cases.

'Hi, Bill,' I began, 'um, are we supposed to sit in the shade sipping a latte and watching them work?' Behind Bill I could see one guy tightening his back brace, trucks were pulling up and everyone was talking into two-way headsets and phones at the same time with both hands full of gear.

'Yup, you're the talent, that's the way it works.'

I was already backing my wet arse towards crisp canvas about to say, 'Fair enough, Bill, I'll have a double Macallan 18, no ice, a number five Montecristo and today's *Sydney Morning Herald*, please, my good man,' but Mat spoke first. 'No, no, we'll jump in and help,' so we did.

The next location was just plain funny. After their research department had pinpointed as best they could the exact place where the First Fleet pitched their tents on the first night, we replicated that as well. As convict I prepared the first meal followed by the first spew. Considering the state of the food left onboard after almost a year at sea, you can imagine the choice was a bit rough. Dead weevils, rotten once-salted beef, pork or mutton, dried peas, flour, cornmeal and water all makes good glue but would've tasted like shit.

The governor chose this spot to make camp because there was a naturally occurring water source coming up through the ground on the western side of what is now Hyde Park. The water formed a natural channel to the cove down present-day Market and King streets in the city. There was a drought in 1789 so reservoirs or 'tanks' for storing the water were cut into the sandstone sides of the channel. Called Tank Stream, it was the new colony's primary source of water for the next 40 years; as Sydney grew the stream became an open drain and by the 1930s it had turned into a stormwater drain. The whole great modern city now sits directly above Tank Stream, and it's still there, still accessible in a section running a diagonal line near the corner of Pitt and Hunter streets. A 225-year-old time capsule preserved.

Russell and Eliot wandered over in the afternoon sun, so very casual, relaxed, all-in-a-day's-work-and-shit; I was still trying to get my head around what they'd already achieved that morning. It wasn't just Mat and I working that day, the other two presenters were filming with other crews as well. While we were rowing into that cruise liner, Giovanna was in a two-seater submarine looking at a Japanese mini-sub that came into Sydney Harbour during World War Two and Andrew was climbing over the Harbour Bridge. We'd also been told that at some point later in the day one of us was going to get strapped into a personal jet pack and sent into the harbour to fly about 8 metres in the air over the water. Tethered via a big hose connected to a powerful mobile floating pump, the presenter would literally fly about like Buzz Light-year. I prayed it wouldn't be me.

For this next shot, though, Mat and I walked down an alleyway following an official from Sydney Water to a nondescript recessed concrete stairway that ended at an ominous-looking steel and wood door. Mat and I were about to enter the bowels of the city. The Tank Stream had not been a sewer for a very long time, but what's down there was far more terrifying than long gone poo. The squeezer ratio had doubled; Sydney Water were right on their game and very organised. We needed all kinds of permission and permits to get down there and it had to be ventilated for eight hours prior to our arrival. We entered a large room just below the surface with benches and rows of safety gear neatly hung on hooks in order of size. It was very nicely done, a bit *Better Homes & Gardens* The Bunker Edition. After a detailed briefing from our guide and another one from Russell on the shots he wanted to get, we accessed the Tank Stream via a vertical shaft through a hatch inside a small room at one end of the bunker. 'If there's a sudden storm, this will fill up to the top in seconds, so we need to be ready,' our guide reminded us.

It was a perfectly round tunnel, big enough to stand up in places, carved out by hand by convicts of the First Fleet, each individual tool strike leaving a pockmarked surface stretching into the black damp recesses beyond the reach of my torchlight. It was quiet down there, with a palpable sense of history. We moved slowly through the tunnel, following the trickle of clear water flowing down the centre. It was clean, there was no bad smell or debris, nothing offensive, until we got to the narrowest point at the end.

I shone my torch ahead of me and leant forward to look. 'Why are the walls moving?'

'Oh, it's just a few roaches,' I heard someone say behind me.

Everyone has a thing, it might be snakes or rats or spiders or poodles. Mine is cockroaches, because years ago I woke from a drunken sleep to discover I had one deep inside my right ear, and it made me crazy. I ended up in hospital screaming and twitching in time to its death throes while a doctor sat on me and a nurse injected oil into my ear.

Every hair on my neck stood up, my ear canals tried to close, film crews and squeezers were scattered and Mat got trampled as I fled towards street level. Now that's what you call talent.

I'll stop there—so much more happened, and that was just the first episode.

SPEED WEEK 3. 2013

THE LAST TIME I saw the BDM-SLS it was rolling back into its trailer on Corowa's main runway in March 2012. I was so sure I would never see her again, at least not in the form of a motorcycle.

I was wrong; somehow, I don't know how, she had remained intact, quietly tucked away in a corner for a full year. I had not heard from Colin, Rob or Ed; we had all been so busy with our lives none of us realised the Dry Lakes Racers Association was successfully granted permission to run Speed Week on the salt a month earlier than usual, and that the salt was in good condition. But more importantly, it had not rained in months and did not look likely to.

David Hinds from the DLRA called me to ask why he hadn't heard from us and whether we were going to the salt this year.

I was sitting in my car about to drive out of a multi-storey car park in the city. I froze. 'Yup, Dave, I'll see you there.'

Several phone calls later the whole thing cranked into life for the third time. We only had two weeks to prepare, but after two years of trying to make it to Speed Week we had the prep side down to a fine art.

So Speed Week 2013 looked like it might actually happen this time. I drove out into the sun feeling euphoric; salt fever would arrive next like a freight train. Those two weeks passed fast: the boys dusted off the bike and reported nothing whatsoever was amiss; I filled out my paperwork, booked flights and pulled out the 25-year-old racing leathers Erwin had lent me last year and gave them a good rub down with beeswax and lanolin. I also pulled out my new gloves, replaced after poor Diego lost one last year, and of course that carbon helmet, now cleaned of Erwin's manky dog's urine. I had spent two weeks working on it only because I knew I'd be in trouble out there on the salt in 50-degree heat in a black helmet trying to concentrate on riding and not the acrid smell of dog piss. I walked about under the sun in my backyard with the visor down and the vents closed, smelling only cleaning chemicals that made me slightly dizzy, but not piss. It was completely pee-free.

The night before my early flight to Adelaide I carefully

packed my gear into a big hold-all bag, going over everything. My kit was laid out on the floor in the garage so I could systematically check it, pack it and know it'd be ready when I needed it. Sid was quietly playing with my socket set as he often did when I was working on a bike or just tinkering in the garage. He had just turned two and was bang in the middle of 'potty training'— or 'helmet training', because it made no difference to him where he took a shit—and he did, just like that. I was distracted 20 feet away with my head in a storage box looking for rechargeable batteries when the chain of events, which I'd lined up to let happen, joined the dots in my head.

First it was a little grunt, followed by the smell; I knew before I turned around what I was going to see. Take one post-spaghetti-bolognaise-fed toddler, place padded comfy-looking receptacle within range, in this case my clean lid sitting hollow side up and supported on all sides, for protection in transit, on top of my leathers and boots, then simply turn your back and let it happen. Sid was not wearing a nappy and, unlike his sister who was very good at announcing her intentions, he simply gave you a three-second warning before he defecated on the spot. So we always had his potty within his window, but this time his potty was not in the garage, so he just improvised and went ahead and backed one out in my lid. 'Daddy, ka ka,' his little voice came seconds later. I turned around and, yes, there he was, bless him.

I didn't react, I just picked him up and carried him into the bathroom and cleaned him up. We walked back down to the garage together and he went quietly back to playing with my socket set while I dropped a thousand dollars of carbon-fibre helmet into a plastic bag and threw it in the bin.

On the final approach into Adelaide, I started going through all the things that would happen next: the phone calls, messages and emails telling me Speed Week was cancelled when I got off the plane. But not this time. This time Rob Dempster was there to pick me up and we drove over to his place near the city and spent the afternoon packing up his four-wheel drive for the four days on the salt. Rob was very generously taking his own vehicle, and thank god he's a four-wheel-drive enthusiast.

I stood sweating under the tin roof of his man cave in the suburbs, slightly bemused at the amount of kit he began pulling off shelves. He handed me a cold beer as soon as I walked in then pulled out a checklist from his shirt pocket and scanned the expanse of his shed. 'Mate, we can't cop a squat out there can we?' he asked. Picking up a twelve-pack of toilet paper and folding shovel with a flat face and a vicious-looking serrated edge, he snapped and twisted its parts together then urgently paced up the row of shelves, rather like a man in dire need of a poop or about to engage in some trench warfare. 'Right, that's the dunny.' He slid a huge grip bag across the floor. 'There are no toilets out there, right?' he asked.

'Well, as far as I know there's toilets on the salt in the pit lane, but nothing in the camp, or perhaps there's a couple in the camp . . .

He laughed. 'Well, you're gonna want to use this one—it's a proper sit-down comfortable rig with its own tent and aircon.'

I suspected he was pulling my leg but was amazed nonetheless. 'Really?'

'Yup.' He walked over with another grip bag. 'Here, take this out to the car.' Soon there were a dozen bags lined up, all clearly marked; the man had everything. Rob takes his off-road adventures seriously, as the inside of his Pajero revealed. He had the whole thing custom-ised with storage areas, collapsible tables, bladders for potable and grey water, full comms, navigation, shade awnings, solar panels, fridges and a butler.

Several beers later we were packed. Ed and Colin were meeting us at the uni first thing in the morning with the bike and the Commodore to tow it, then we had to swing by Steve Smith's place and pick him up before a four-hour drive to Port Augusta, refuel and on to Iron Knob another hour southwest. Just outside Iron Knob there was a turn-off on the right on a dirt road; another three hours down that and we'd be at the lake.

Steve is one of the machinists at the uni. He's short with a round belly, a greying goatee and an impossibly funny nature, he's an Aussie male in the old-school, man's man sense. You know, he'll build a car in his shed, weld something, gas-axe something else, bash something with a big fuck-off hammer, shoot something, mow the lawn, drink a carton, then jump online and move some shares around at a tidy profit all before lunchtime.

Steve's man cave was just like Rob's, full of cars in various stages of undress, classic motorcycles beautifully restored, and tools, so many tools. Their caves had the same smell, motor oil mixed with paint and musty canvas with a dash of whiskey, like catching a passing whiff of Old Spice while doing an oil change. It should be turned into a cologne called 'Sure Root' and put in a bottle shaped like a football. Brad Pitt should do the ad, wearing comedy breasts and tossing his hair while sitting on a Holden, and they should shoot the whole thing in Steve's shed. Brad should do it for free just to get his man cred back from Chanel, except this time he won't get to drink the product before they start shooting. I used to work in advertising, part time, and I never comment on ads, well, apart from almost everything in the chapter called 'Advertising', but that particular commercial and the millions they spent to ultimately shit on a wonderful product that my mother uses as well as poor Brad—well, it was just bizarre to watch. Like fly-kicking your grandmother, once is enough.

We pulled away from Steve's place, Rob and I in his Pajero with Colin, Ed and Steve in the Commodore pulling the bike trailer. The cars had UHF radios so as soon as we hit the highway the banter started between

Colin and Rob, and didn't stop all the way to the turn-off outside Iron Knob. We hooked up the Pajero to tow the trailer and entered the 130-kilometre bush track full of anticipation.

The DLRA had their first meeting to race on the salt here in 1990; 25 people turned up with less than ten cars to race, and only two of the cars were purpose-built salt-racing cars. Now there are almost a thousand members and most of them were already at the lake when we arrived. This is a sport, a motorsport unlike any other. It takes real commitment, and you need to be focused and very patient—just getting out to the event is a massive effort.

Dry lake racing's origins go back to the 'hot rodders' of the 1930s and guys who beefed up their cars to drag-race them, basically anywhere they could. This evolved into competitive drag-racing. In the post-war boom the money racers spent on their cars and motorcycles jumped up and as a result so too did their speed, leaving the Southern Californian Timing Association looking for an official venue big enough to race safely on. This became the first official Speed Week at Bonneville in 1949, but the place was used by racers way before that. The first race that's remembered involved a car and a train. The train tracks cross Bonneville for more than 200 kilometres, so in 1927 a Salt Lake City local raced his Studebaker against a Union Pacific locomotive. Eight years later the British racer Sir Malcolm Campbell cracked 300 mph on the salt.

That first year of Speed Week must have been amazing, the thin mountain air in Utah's northwestern corner crackling as the first racers put the hammer down. They just adopted a 'run-what-you-brung' philosophy that has now evolved into more than 70 different categories—just for cars, with about the same number again for bikes—and within those classes there are multiple subdivisions broken down through engine capacity, fuel, fuel management, frames, fairings, the list goes on. So you can stand on the salt pan and watch a 60-year-old woman set a land-speed record riding a 1950s Triumph that's completely clapped out with a top speed of 100 kph, but in that particular class, it's a new record. Then she can make some minor changes to the bike, re-enter in another class and set another record. It's progressive and exciting, and soon there will be more: the world's fastest lawnmower, golf cart, sewing machine, combine harvester—as long as it's safe and there's a motor in it, eventually there will be a class that fits the bill in some way, shape or form. So you don't have to be some minted ultra-slick rocket-car-driving corporate giant, anyone can have a go.

Having said that, however, we didn't fit in and were in a new no-man's-land on the salt. We had a motorcycle, but it had a car engine in it, and we were also running our bike on bio-diesel so it fell into more strange uncharted areas as there was only one other diesel motorcycle at the event. No electric motorcycles turned up or other bikes running anything outside the norm in terms of combustion. So according to the rules we were officially 'unclassified', neither a car nor a bike, so whatever we did out there would also be unrecognised officially. I'm sure other bikes will be built and one day there will be a class we can fit into.

Rob let out a 'Woooo!' as we rounded a corner and got our first glimpse of the salt.

'Fuck, it's big,' he said.

'Fuck, it's white,' said Steve over the radio.

We pulled up at the entrance to the camp. 'Fuck, it's hot,' said Colin as he got out of the air-conditioned Holden. We had a good look around the DLRA camp. It was right next to the salt, so we picked a spot near some trees, rigged up our shade and Rob's James Bond toilet complete with aircon unit, night light, toilet roll holder and selection of reading material, all of which constituted the same 40 pages of fart jokes, photographs of drunk people vomiting on each other, visual puzzles that involved matching various augmented breasts to their famous owners, with the prize for the lucky winner a motorised esky with flames emblazoned down both sides, and a crossword puzzle Helen Keller could finish. We laid out our swags, disconnected the trailer, and opened the back to check on the bike.

The inside was completely caked in red dust; it looked like a paprika bomb just went off. So we cleaned it up, checked it over and cruised down to the salt for our first look.

GOT SALT?

IT WAS WINDING down for the day. Everyone was off the salt at five and not allowed back on until sun-up, then the tracks opened at seven. The 'pit lane' was made up of two rows of team sites, one after another, about 50 metres apart, extending for a few hundred metres. It was a strange sight, these two parallel rows of self-made workshops sitting in the middle of a Dulux-white flat plain that extended into the horizon.

We walked slowly down the lane taking it all in. The rattle of pneumatic tools and laughter from one side mixed with the sudden roar of a big-block V8 firing up on the other side; music bellowed from a old bus converted into a mobile tool shed; a guy wearing only a sombrero, a pair of budgie-smugglers and a high-vis vest scooted past us on a minibike singing a Creedence song. There was an instant sense of community, of comradeship; everyone wandered about like it was a giant family barbecue. Random racers I'd never met before in my life knew who I was and would greet me like an old mate; they knew we had been waiting for three years for this opportunity, just like they had, and made me feel welcome instantly.

Genuine interest and a common goal prevailed as an undercurrent, like an invisible subterranean river running under the salt and permeating through every conversation, every wave and curious nod towards your bike or car or rocket. Not one person was going to walk up to me over the next four days and say, 'Mate, is that thing diesel?' They just knew, and their questions were often at a level that only Colin or Ed could answer. Blokes that looked like they literally just got out of prison for eating babies would wander up, crack a massive smile and say something like, 'Good afternoon, gents, tell me, what's the in-line velocity resistance like on that super tipex 5000 G-Spot pulse injector modulator in this temperature, cos mine's running like shit today.' And I would just go blank.

Everyone knew their stuff, inside out, upside down, back to front, and everyone had an exploded diagram of every part of their machine in their heads at all times. I was lost like a cocktail waitress in a G8 summit and left the pit lane a little in awe. But, as I soon learnt, there's a very good reason why these people are so tuned up, because if it gets gnarly out there you're a long way from medical help or a mechanical workshop.

That evening after Rob's campsite culinary skills produced an excellent dish cleverly called 'Rob's Surprise'—an amalgamation of pasta and sauce mixed with several nondescript forms of grey genuine imitation meat substitutes—I grabbed a whiskey and wandered over to the edge of the lake to watch the sun go down. It was so beautiful, a warm kaleidoscope of changing colours sliding across the sheen of the salt as the sun melted into the horizon, it could have been an alien planet, then the stars came out clear and bright. I walked back to our camp, hearing laughter and conversation all around; this was a new sensation, experiencing this blend of awe, excitement and belonging.

I was sitting down on a folding chair, our camp lit by the headlights of Rob's four-wheel drive, when a filthy bloke in work gear reeking of oil and madness leapt out from the night. My mate Simon Hann had jumped into a site vehicle and driven nonstop from a drilling rig in the middle of Queensland. After the relief of not having crapped ourselves because of his little prank, we were all suitably excited to see him.

Steve had never met Simon so I introduced them as Steve stepped out of Rob's luxuriously appointed bush shower wrapping a towel round his belly. 'Where the fuck did you just come from?' Steve said as he shook Simon's hand.

'I just drove down from a drilling location in Queensland,' Simon explained.

'Ah, you're in the drilling game,' Steve said, nodding to himself in confirmation, 'I thought I could smell the booze.'

We were soon all settled around our camp under Pajero headlights, talking rubbish and pissing ourselves laughing while working our way through a vintage Macallan liberated from my father's stash—cheers, Dad.

Monday morning 6 a.m. Rob woke me by undoing the little zippered flap door on my swag and farting through the opening. 'Rise and shine, speed racer.' He laughed and staggered over to his bush shower. But I knew he wouldn't be laughing for long. Last night after we'd finished off 'Rob's Surprise' I got my first go in Rob's James Bond racing toilet, unfortunately forgetting that there was a series of valves to open and levers to pump prior to leaving the remains of 'Rob's Surprise', so I just left it for Rob, as a surprise. As he entered, you could hear him swearing from the pit lane.

Day one for us was the rookie drivers' meeting; this involved getting the breakdown on pre-qualification to run our vehicle on the main timed track. Speed Week has two tracks: the main timed track and a GPS 3-mile track where you run your machine for the first time on the salt. The GPS track, as the name suggests, is not officially timed; instead they use GPS units to log your speed. It's also used to qualify for your various licences.

The categories were as follows:

- Category E, current and valid state driver's licence
- Category D, 125 to 149 mph
- Category C, 150 to 174 mph
- Category B, 175 to 199 mph
- Category A, 200 to 249 mph
- Category AA, 250 to 299 mph
- Unlimited, 300 mph and faster.

The record, albeit unofficial, that we were chasing was set in 2007 at Bonneville by a Texan man running a custom-built bike with a BMW 3 Series car engine; he reached 130.614 mph (210.203 kph). So if I was successful in qualifying for my first licence Category D, I'd have the opportunity to break his record.

We towed the trailer down onto the salt and set about rigging up our pit lane digs. Once we got the shade frame up and a large tarp down, we secured everything to the salt with big tech screws and homemade plywood rings like washers, because at night the wind rips across the lake with enough force to blow your entire camp away. The daytime heat is brutal: the average temperature is 50 degrees Celsius, there's no natural shade or water, and everything is bleached white so the heat is bounced and radiated from above and below. It's dangerous enough going fast on an uneven unsealed surface; out there it felt like we were doing that on the surface of the sun, and I hadn't even got my leathers on yet.

The meeting for us rookies was held by a gentleman simply and universally called 'Animal', who reared up out of nowhere and grabbed a microphone. The huge crowd instantly fell silent, especially us 'Salt Virgins', as Animal cleared his throat. Standing on the step of the DLRA mobile office, he sported shorts, thongs, a high-vis vest and a huge handlebar moustache that almost covered his mouth, basically looking like he would kill anyone who didn't pay attention. So we all paid attention.

Next was scrutineering or tech inspection, where the DLRA officials make sure that your vehicle is good to go. The rulebook is thick and very detailed so this isn't a hasty process. I jumped on the bike and rode it over to the three-lane queue forming for inspection. The vehicles that started lining up looked incredible and their noise alone vibrated right through my body: fully retro-styled hotrods, cigar-tube Lakesters with mirror-polished giant wheels jutting out that looked like full-size 1950s toy cars, the full spec Streamliners ready to push 300 mph, a Jaguar E type and an XJS, a 356 Porsche Speedster—there was even an old split-windscreen Volkswagen Kombi in there, and a truck. The bikes were equally diverse and abundant, from a Honda CT 110 postie bike capable of more than 80 mph to vintage to ultra-modern, the lot.

I bounced around the three queues talking to everyone and getting their take on racing on the salt, and enjoyed the same mix of smiles and heatstroke. However, the scrutineering gets serious when you consider the speed these people are reaching; it gets even more serious when you see the inside of their vehicles and watch them go through the inspection process.

One by one they demonstrated that they could 'bail out', which sounds like they're going to jump from their vehicles or something but actually means they know how to save themselves. If you're hurtling across the salt at warp speed and something goes very wrong, you need to have the presence of mind to remove your death grip from the steering wheel, pull the parachute, kill the master switch, activate the fire extinguishers, kill the fuel pump and start the process of egress from your fully armoured driver seat, assuming you're not upside down or on fire and are still conscious, possibly having just flipped over several thousand times. Getting out is even harder.

You know that old footage of the manned rocket missions into outer space in the 60s and the astronaut with his briefcase air supply is getting helped into his seat, then the German guys in the lab coats pile into the capsule and strap the astronaut in by standing on his groin and shoulders and pulling collectively as hard as they can. Well, these salt lake racing guys are strapped in like that, so they can just breathe, then their entire full-face-helmet-clad head is restrained and strapped into another metal frame, then their arms are tethered with more straps and they're also wearing fireproof undies, dragster spec fire suit and gloves.

As I stood there I suddenly realised that Speed Week is a serious and extremely dangerous business.

By the time we got to the scrutineering tent I was grinning but completely terrified, I had also managed to cook my brain and was overheating at a frightening rate. The motorcycle scrutineer looked at my riding gear and helmet, then turned to Ed and asked if I'd recently had a stroke. 'Mate, you need to drink some water and try to relax before your run,' he said to me.

I nodded but couldn't talk as I'd run out of spit and my tongue was stuck to the roof of my mouth.

'The bike's fine,' he said and slapped my pass into my hand. 'Good luck.'

He smiled and moved on to the next bike, while we went back to our pits where I drank 600 litres of water, pulled on my leathers and boots and got in the queue at the back of the GPS track.

Speed Week is all about queuing and patience and drinking 600 litres of water and still not peeing. At the GPS track a truly oddball mix of would-be speed aficionados lined up, sitting around in leathers in 50-degree heat and waiting their go. Mates, wives and family members took it in turns to hold umbrellas over heads while now and again someone would pour water down the back of racing leathers, wet towels abundant. We patiently waited for our turn while Ed ferried water to me. I needed a nappy by the time I was at the pre-start line.

CRAZY PAVING

FINALLY THE PRE-START line was there in front of me; about 10 metres beyond that lay the start line, a thin length of blue rope stretched across the surface of the salt. This was when I had a few moments to get organised while the rider ahead of me waited for the official starter to give him the nod. I waited with the bike grumbling under me while sweat trickled down under my leathers; helmet on and strapped, engine on, fuel pump, fuel management system, engine kill line tethered to my wrist, GPS, gloves, all on.

Sean Kelly was the man ahead of me. He was poised, focused and ready, and the starter was standing to Sean's left with a two-way radio pressed against his ear waiting for the spotters down the track to tell him it was all clear.

Then Sean rolled forward slightly and collapsed, falling from his bike; the engine died the moment his hand left the grip. The starter rushed in to get his helmet off. Sean was in trouble and was whisked away into the shade, his bike pushed over to one side.

The starter waved me forward. I popped the bike into gear and rolled up to the line and looked down the endless track; the Coriolis effect of the earth came into play here. The lake was so vast, I was suddenly not hot anymore—I was so pumped I nearly puked pure adrenalin into my lid. I broke my stare into the white abyss to look over at the starter; he was talking into the two-way, then he stopped, gave me a big smile. 'Good to go,' he shouted over the engine noise. 'Visor down,' he motioned like a man finishing a salute and pointed down the track. 'Go!'

I throttled on slowly and clutched out at the same rate, remembering I had so much more time and space than the blacktop, this was the salt. The bike still slid slightly sideways, fishtailing off the line with wheel spin through first gear. Second stopped the slide and I gained grip and acceleration, slowly climbing through the revs. It's a bizarre surface to ride on, the whole lake looks like white crazy paving. It's not a flat smooth surface at all; each piece of the crazy paving is at a slightly differ-ent angle from the one it's attached to, and in between there is a bulbous line of salt that grows out of the cracks like too much mortar between concrete slabs. The track is about 10 metres wide and visible because the DLRA shave the salt mortar off the surface in the morning by dragging a huge piece of angle iron down the track.

Third gear started the vibrations, to my horror, that increased to a point where I could no longer read my instruments. The boundary between the salt and sky blurred on the horizon as I found fourth gear and tucked in as hard as I could. That morning I lay on the surface near our pits and licked the lake while Simon laughed at me; it tasted like salt, it looked like salt. I rubbed it between my fingers and imagined hitting it at 200 mph with a half-tonne bike on my head. It was tacky to the touch and sticky underfoot, caking onto shoes and tyres. But now in the heat it had dried out and hardened; now it was like a combination of hard damp sand and snow. The 1-mile marker shot past my shoulder out of the blinding white blur, then from nowhere a massive gust of wind hit the bike and shunted it over to the left; adrenalin made me grip harder and heave the bike into the wind, trying to correct my line. Inexperience had me riding down the centre of the track and not prepared for the crosswind at the halfway mark that everyone, even the guy selling meat pies off the back of his ute in the pit lane, knew about, except me.

The unique composition of the salt and the power of the wind combined with the size of my bike meant that although I was leaning as hard as I could into the wind, I was still getting pushed and sliding across the surface closer to the left edge of the track. Straying off the track meant a fall. I backed off the throttle and regained control. Salt lake racing was not at all what I imagined it would be like. I thought it would be easy, you just hold on and go, but it's not that simple.

My ride down the return track ended at the back of the queue where the DLRA officials retrieved their GPS unit and logged your speed. The official said, '94.6 mph,' and went on to the next vehicle. That's about 152 kph, well under what I'd achieved on the tar and much less than what we knew the bike was capable of.

Ed and Colin looked perplexed. With few words exchanged we put the bike in the pits and then I hit up every rider I could find over the next few hours, getting the rundown on speed and wind and salt.

The first question they asked me was always 'What are you riding?'. After I told them, the same sympathetic face was pulled. I found Jeff Lemon, a big New Zealander, very experienced rider and record holder. Jeff knows salt lake racing; he does Speed Week both here and at Bonneville. With that classic, quiet, methodical all-in-a-day's-racing calm about him, he jumps on his bike and sets a record as casually as I would nip down to the supermarket for a loaf of bread. Jeff was on the verge of cracking the 'Dirty Two'—that means passing 200 mph—on a stock Suzuki. He smiled when I found him; he knew I'd just had my first run and had been waiting for the onslaught of questions. 'When the crosswind hit you, did you go rigid and get the death grip on the handlebars?'

I nodded.

'Did the bike slide to the left?'

I nodded.

'Were you running down the centre of the track?'

More nodding; he talked and I listened.

'When that crosswind catches you, don't panic,' Jeff said. 'Whatever you do, don't sit up—just a shoulder poking out from your fairing can throw your bike off balance and cause a fall. So just relax into it, crank your steering damper right up, tuck in and steer the bike, don't go rigid and over-grip. That bike presents a huge surface area for the wind to push against and you're running solid wheels, so you need all that track to get up to speed because it's big and heavy. It's a lottery: you either ride through it or you need a run with no crosswind.'

My bike had been granted an exemption for the solid wheels; just having solid wheels is enough in a crosswind to blow a bike off the track, as opposed to a spoked wheel which allows the wind to pass through it. The rules stated that front wheels had to be cross-ventilated by an area equal to at least 25 per cent of normal rim circle area, but my bike was outside the rules and required me to compensate accordingly out on the salt.

Jeff put his big hand on my shoulder and leant in to speak over the noise of V8 crackling nearby. 'Start your run at the far right of the track and try to stay there, the cars and other vehicles are churning up the surface and dumping loose salt on the left side, that should give you more time to get speed before the wind just blows that huge mainsail with wheels off the track.' He slapped me on the back and laughed. 'Go and catch some wisdom out there as well as crosswind. Now get back in the queue.'

I went back to the pits and talked to the lads. First we put more air into the tyres, an overpressure of 20 psi; this would help any correcting lean against the wind. Jeff told me not to worry about there being less tyre surface contact with the salt as I'd have so much forward momentum keeping me upright. Next we cut off the back of the front wheel guard; it was creating drag. Ed buried his head in the computer fuel management system, tweaking the software around the extreme heat to get more from the hardware, and with that I was back in my leathers and sitting in the queue again.

I asked another rider next to me if he knew what had happened to Sean Kelly. 'Heat stroke, mate,' he said. So I drank another 600 litres of water over the next 40 minutes until I found myself at the pointy end of the queue again. Sean Kelly had been put in a special shower that is set up for racers to recover from heat stroke; he got out of there and went on to smash two world records, and drink 600 litres of water.

LIVING CRAZY TO CATCH WISE

AS FAR AS Speed Week goes, it's 90 per cent waiting and 10 per cent racing.

'How'd you go?' The starter at the GPS track yelled at me, smiling with his big hat on.

I smiled back in my helmet and gave him the thumbs-up. 'Can I go over to the right?'

He nodded. 'Crosswind?'

I shifted over slightly to the right, primed myself and the bike, gave the starter the nod.

'Stand by . . . Visor down . . . *Go!*'

Exactly the same thing happened again, at the same point: the crosswind collected me, but this time I held on the power, leant into the wind way past my comfort zone and held my breath, letting go on the power as the bike wobbled through the loose salt in the middle and slid towards the left edge. I remembered not to sit up or touch the brakes and changed down very late to avoid a compression lock on the back wheel. The result was 95.5 mph, 153 kph.

I rode in to the back of the queue. Everyone was suffering from the extreme heat and dealing with the wind in their own way. I sat there thinking about it: all the things I took for granted when riding this bike on the asphalt on that runway at Corowa last year were now amplified on the salt to a new and utterly frightening degree. That kind of speed on a factory racing bike, on a straight racetrack, is child's play, but on a half-tonne, homemade, 4-metre-long behemoth, on this surface, with this crosswind, and the aerodynamics of a Sherman tank, I started to realise Jeff was right. This was a lottery, a flat-out gamble on whether or not I could hold onto the power through the wind and stay on the track long enough to nail it. It was that simple.

Salt fever was creeping in, that heady mix of adrenalin and fear; I now knew why these nutters kept coming back. Their source code was written, processed and hard-wired into their brain the second they finished their first run. It takes years to get the feel for what you're doing out there. Lake Gairdner is widely recognised as being just as good as Bonneville, the slightly fat but funny little sister of the queen of speed in the USA. As I rolled towards my third run, she reminded me that although fun to be around, and good to look at, she's got gas, and can ruin your day if you don't give her the respect she deserves. It was at this moment she blew one of her 30 kph crosswinds at the queue and half a dozen riders stack it, including me.

Embarrassed by this, everyone sprang up and immediately heaved their bikes off the ground. It took four guys to get mine back on two wheels and, unbeknown to me at the time, I had just fractured my L5 vertebra; that is to say, a half-tonne bike falling on you is going to hurt and it did, but I did what men do and ate painkillers to shake it off.

Half a box of Tramadol later I was back at the start line; the starter, still grinning, jogged over. 'You again, we need to stop meeting like this.' He leant in to remind me of the gusting crosswind somewhere after the first mile and asked if I was sure I wanted to make a run. I nodded and flicked my visor down.

Pulling away off the line, I was racing myself; I'm my own worst enemy and always have been. My back spasmed as I tucked in, my movements through the clutch lever, gear lever, throttle twist now automatic. I wasn't shooting fast glances down at gauges; I could hear the rpm, I could feel what the bike was doing. My death grip was now just a loose hold, and everything was focused on the vibrating horizon, its fixed, fully charged dark clouds colliding high above and sparking lightning across the windscreen. When the first mile marker blipped past my peripheral left I was flat out in fourth gear; any moment now that fucking crosswind would hit me. What do you do? Definitive moments, life comes down to them all the time. Fiddle with your comfort levels, your life, your sanity; if you don't you will always wonder. I let out a high-speed torrent of abuse, shouting as hard and loud as I could while my mind dropped acid and decided to show me pictures of Lola and Sid hugging my father. The wind slammed into the side of the bike, the handlebars wobbled, and there was a sharp intake of breath as I made leaning corrections, pulling the bike over further than I dared and slipping into the mushy centre of the track.

My point of no return had already passed in third gear. I lost my battle as the wind relentlessly shunted me over to the left and that was it—by the time the wind was gone I'd run out of room again; there was no touching the brakes out there and I needed the remaining track to slow down using the gearbox. The second I rolled off the power I knew it was over, I was done. 'Chalk this up to gaining experience, mate,' I told myself. If there was a lesson to catch, I caught it. I caught it between my butt cheeks.

Rolling into the back of the queue I was met with some big smiles—98.2 mph, 158 kph. Colin was beaming from ear to ear. 'That's an Australian record.' He was pumped. I was getting closer to the world record on every run. It was four in the afternoon by then and the lads and I decided to shut it down for the day. Jeff waved to me as we left the salt for our camp and shouted, 'Tomorrow, mate, you'll crack it tomorrow.'

That night it was Simon's Surprise for dinner, and the man can cook. His tent was big enough to hold an air show in; in fact, every single bit of kit he had was emblazoned with his employer's logo, he had just grabbed whatever he could and bolted. The end of that first day of racing had wasted all of us. I fell into an exhausted, blank sleep.

The next day I was crawling out of my swag like Satan himself had put on an oversized ski boot and spent the entire night kicking my lower back. Rob's Breakfast Surprise with a generous side of Tramadol put me in a lucid but slightly wonky state as I pulled on my sweat-soaked leathers in the pits and waited for the drugs to kick in.

There was that massive queue again. With just two tracks open, and most of us restricted to running on the GPS track, 330 racers meant you had to wait, a lot. By 9 a.m. it was already 45 degrees Celsius under that sun. Just as it's getting hard and down to the pointy end, that's when Speed Week will stop you in mid-conversation and leave you standing motionless with your mouth slightly agape while the hairs on your arms stand up as you see, for the first time, a magnificent race spec Streamliner at full tilt hurtling down the main track like a bullet through the heat haze. Its trajectory is bewildering against the white and red background of this place, salt blasted into a vapour trail behind this missile, its massive engine noise out of sync with the speed as you try to wrap your head around the physics and what the driver is experiencing at more than 250 mph. There was a momentary silence as everyone focused completely on this one event and collectively tracked the run, which relaxed only when the chute billowed and the engine noise was gone, then it was straight back to whatever you were doing. It was a definitive Speed Week moment.

'Morning.' The starter was chirpy.

'Crosswind?' I asked.

'Yup, same place,' he said.

Then we went through our little ritual that finished with him yelling 'Go', and so it went on for the rest of the day. I never got past my fastest run of 98.2 mph. By three o'clock my toe and back were fucked and we called it a day.

'Can't do it, Colin.' I fell off the bike and lay on the tarp in our pits, undoing my helmet strap while prone.

'Mate, you managed an Australian record,' Colin said as he eased the helmet off my head. 'That's good enough for your first race meet.'

I lay there looking at the shade sail flapping in the wind. He knew what I was thinking: it wasn't good enough, I wanted the world record. 'Next year,' I said.

Ed came over and pulled my boots off. 'Well done, mate,' he said as he threw my boots in the back of the trailer and helped me up. 'Let's go and have a whiskey.'

We loaded the bike into the trailer and headed down to the main track where only a handful of cars and bikes had qualified to race the full 8 miles. We pulled out deck-chairs and sat on the roof of the trailer with umbrellas, watching the show.

And what a show it was. One car flipped at over 150 mph; its nose lifting and swapping ends mid-air, it smashed its way down the track several times while we stood on the roof frozen. The driver was pulled out with only eight-ball haemorrhages in his eyes, other than that he was fine. The safety procedures at Speed Weed work. But I was amazed that his first bounce covered 130 metres in distance, and totally floored when the driver announced he was ready to get back in and do it again.

I watched other bike riders get hit by that potentially lethal crosswind and get the wobbles on, sliding all over the track at more than 200 mph, then regain control and hammer on. There were a few who came off, but they all walked away. Well, except for the two guys who came off their bikes on the way home; one broke his neck, the other his femur.

By the time the event was over there was a total of 641 runs logged, with 72 records set—38 new ones and 34 existing records broken—and 21 men joined the Dirty Two club. Me, well, I didn't do what I intended to, but I got a good taste.

We left the salt the next morning. Jeff Lemon was standing in his bush shower as we drove past on our way out of camp, his head covered in soap. 'Catch ya next year, mate,' he shouted.

I looked at Colin, quiet in the back seat. 'Will he?' I asked.

'Yeah, we'll work it out somehow, Pauli.' He smiled. 'But you need to ride like hell next time.'

LIKE CARTER, LIKE SON

IT'S EARLY IN the morning: the kids are still asleep, Clare is in the kitchen making coffee. I hear the phone ring inside and walk in through the back door. 'It's your sister.' Clare looks worried and hands over the phone.

My father is dying. His optimistic phone banter has been so convincing these past months, but now I'm listening to my sister tell me he's losing his battle.

She is in tears, and reveals that my father is holding on to meet my son. Anyone in my position would drop everything, gather their family together and get on the next flight to London. I dump several things on Maximum Dave, both work and personal; he even collects the mail and mows the lawn while we're gone.

The Olympics are about to wind down, introducing a state of chaos for everything from booking flights to getting a hotel room, so I give my good mate Shane Edwards—Fast Eddy—a call. As usual, he is spectacular; in a day he has the lot set up like clockwork, even transport from Heathrow to the Hilton, which he's chosen for its location across the street from Paddington station and the train to Cheltenham where my mother and sister would pick us up. He has also squared away a car with child seats and a ground floor apartment just 2 miles away from my father's house; how he does this in the lead-up to the Cheltenham horseracing season I don't know, but that's why he's Fast Eddy.

We board our flight in a state of limbo, the beginning of what is basically a series of queues; for the next 36 hours we will be in a queue of one form or another. For once, our kids are controllable, Sid only occasionally throwing food at the other passengers, Lola happy to just sit and draw or watch the TV. By the time we land in London 24 hours later they are both exhausted and asleep. Eddy's driver is there and soon we are all passed out in a hotel room.

The end of a long warm English summer has London's streets bathed in sunshine and a few hundred thousand punters spilling in and out of Paddington station. We jostle our way through the ticketing machine queue while Sid decides to lick every possible surface his head can reach all the way to our seats.

Cheltenham lies two hours down the track northwest

of London. Sitting there on the train, my blank face pointing out the window as rural Britain went by, the familiar deep green patchwork and ancient hedgerows blur seamlessly into the memory of the last time I saw my dad. Almost a year ago, standing in the Gloucestershire sun on the platform at Cheltenham station, seeing me off. He knew then that he was very sick, and I suppose I felt it, the sense that there was something wrong, but I let my life batter its way into my radar and scramble the message before I understood it. Now as we coast into the same station, in the same light, I can picture him there, waiting, his hands shoved into his pockets and a big bearded smile creeping across his face. This time, though, it's my mother, looking fabulous, who I see first when we arrive, she's there with my sister, France, my stepfather, John and my brother-in-law, Barry.

The scene is a happy one, but I know we're going straight to my father's house and I'm going to get a shock. Elisabeth, my father's partner for more than twenty years, answers the door; she's the most remarkable woman, not only because she was able to control my dad. She was also in the Royal Air Force and outranked him before retiring from a long and distinguished military career. I think it is her resolve and inner strength that inspires me more than anything else while dealing with this, a parent's death. You know that in the normal order of things this will one day happen, but you're never prepared for it when it does.

Dad is up and smartly dressed, half his normal body weight and ravaged by the cancer, his face grey and drawn.

He was a big powerful man once, now I can lift him off the sheets. He has two visits with us and the kids, soaking up every second with Lola and Sid; although drawn and sunken, his eyes light up when his grandchildren hug him and chat the way little children do. It takes every ounce of strength he has to get up and be there for us.

Five days later I'm there at the house. It's late, past midnight, when I stir from my sleep on the couch and get up to check on dad. Elisabeth is in there with him, of course, as is my sister. I sit on the end of his bed and chat to him; he makes no sound other than laboured breaths. I don't know how much time passes while I talk and Dad's chest moves in a slow, uneven rhythm with his breathing. He leaves us very quietly, just a brief last look, then his eyes close for the final time, and all the while Elisabeth talks to him, her voice so soft and reassuring. After a life that had been at times fraught with danger and so much tension, of which I only know of fragments, he had a peaceful death at home surrounded by his children and his true love.

It's only now that I can start to understand how close life and death are all the time, so much closer than my rational mind can process here in my safe, secure, free western democracy. It takes on a new parallel when it's your immediate family; he was gone, just when our relationship was getting interesting. I step outside into the street with a glass of Dad's Macallan; I found the bottle in his collection, one that I gave him thirteen years ago, still wrapped up, a 1969 vintage, the year I was born.

The house is an old Georgian three-storey right in the centre of town, the wide street in the early morning standing deftly quiet. I pace up and down in the half light of a new sunrise and toast my father. I wonder if Sid will do this one day; my son reminds me of my father more and more each day. I'll hold on to the thought that the soul lives on in memory and the next generation. Now I have moved up the queue, the big queue, that is.

The one thing that I have learnt from this is get prepared, get a life insurance policy, get your will sorted out, get your affairs in order, and your bills paid, and if you're done with some possession, collection, hobby or other accumulative pursuit, get fucking rid of it or leave it specifically covered in said will before you die, if not for tax reasons then just so your family are not suddenly laboured with what to do with, oh, say, a silenced weapon and 500 rounds of subsonic pistol ammunition or a 1964 Commendation for Bravery from HRH the Queen that no one knew about and you'll never get the chance to ask. Or the collection of various passports, or the albums of photographs of people you have never seen before— I could go on. Suffice to say I don't think I even scratched the surface of getting to know who my father really was, I don't think anyone did. He presented a myriad of different versions of himself to suit the particular audience, and somewhere within that stood my father.

I choose a nice two-piece grey suit, his favourite shoes and tie, and we wait for the funeral director to come and collect him. That's a strange time. Elisabeth suggests we lie Dad out straight while he is still flexible. 'It makes the funeral director's job so much easier if he's nice and straight when they get here,' she says, ever thoughtful. So we pull off the bedclothes and get him nice and straight and level, the only problem being when I pull the pillow out from under Dad's head and his mouth opens up. Elisabeth has already left the room; my sister looks at me with this 'What now?' expression and starts crying. 'Go and put the kettle on,' I tell her. 'I'll sort him out,' I say, like I know exactly what I'm doing, and she leaves.

Dad's mouth is wide open, and he had a big mouth, in a physical sense. I lean over and very gently push his jaw up and close it, delicately drawing back and looking down at him; it stays shut for about ten seconds, then pops open again. Now this goes on for a good few minutes, getting slightly harder with each push, and every time when I close Dad's mouth he begins to have a slight smile on closing, just a hint at first, but it was definitely a smile by the time I start losing it. I prop a pillow under his chin, then a cushion, I try a book, I go into his closet, pour another glass of scotch and come out with one of his neckties and stand there talking to him. 'Look, mate, just help me out here, for Christ's sake,' and I down my drink and tie his jaw up with a nice bow at the top, and pop, his mouth opens up again. I try a belt, pop, another tie, pop, two ties, pop, two ties and the belt, pop. Another scotch and I'm eyeballing the stapler on his desk. 'You're loving this shit,' I say and he smiles back at me in that knowing way.

I'm straddling his chest and, with a combination of knotted-together ties, wrapping his head up as fast as humanly possible, knotting the top in a half-hitch as hard as I can, all the while talking to Dad as beads of nervous sweat leave my bald head and land on his, and my sister walks in with a cup of tea, that she drops.

'Paul,' she says, and closes the door behind her then gives me the hushed bollocking at quarter volume. 'What the fuck are you doing?'

My head spins around; her hands are covering her mouth, 'I'm taking him out for breakfast, what the fuck do you think I'm doing?' I say and hop off.

We stand there looking at our father and she grabs the scotch out of my hand and takes a drink.

'He's smiling,' she says.

'Yes, I know,' I reply. Our father lay there with four neckties wrapped around his head, grinning up at us.

'Cheers, Dad, nice one,' France says and leaves us.

The funeral is hard. I am amazed at how many people turn up, as well as the flood of messages, emails and telegrams that come in over the next few days from all over the world. The church is packed. Elisabeth has done an amazing job, organising everything and giving my father a very civilised and memorable send-off. My mother is effortlessly supportive and that makes her such a wonderful mum. Afterwards I stand in the corner at the wake and one by one meet people who knew Dad, people in uniform, in kilts. I'm hit with more than one Masonic handshake and lodge banter, reams of characters, some of them quite teary, and young people who tell me that they wouldn't be where they were in business today without Dad's support. They all talk about a man who they would miss, especially his sense of humour.

Dad went out smiling in the end. He managed to stay on this good earth long enough to hold his grandchildren and tell them how much he loved them. And I got to throttle him with a necktie.

Honi soit qui mal y pense—I found these words on the back of my father's commendation, so small I could barely make them out. They say, 'Evil to him who evil thinks.'

SPECIAL THANKS

After repeated snivelling, I was backed by several companies. Had they not, I would still be sitting on my arse in Perth wondering how fast that bike could have gone, and for that I am truly grateful.

So thanks to Linc Energy, Vallourec & Mannesmann Tubes, SGS Australia, Jet-Lube, Besmindo, Pentagon Freight, Frank's International, Xtex, Test Trak, Prospero Productions, Roadbend Jaguar.

rainwaterhog.com

ACKNOWLEDGEMENTS

Jason Theo, Peter Bond, Shaun Southwell, Erwin Herczeg, Donald Millar, Mark and Elaine Murray, Neil Boath, Ross Luck, Christiaan Durrant, Jethro Nelson, Matt Bromley (still alive after riding into God's blind spot), Howard Fletcher, Simon Hann, Maximum Dave, Clayton Jacobson, Diego Berazategui, Janelle van de Velde, Jim Thompson, Les Ellis, Drew Gardenier, Craig Walding, Gregg and Sherri Cooper, Ashley Taylor, Tony Pecival, Hartley Taylor, the remarkable Elisabeth Sandison, Associate Professor Colin Kestell, Rob Dempster, Ed Styles, Steve Smith, Russell Vines, Eliot Buchan, Ed Punchard, Julia Redwood, Nicole Tetrault, Duncan Milne, Sally and Simon Dominguez, Julian Carraher, Dare Jennings, Jeff Lemon, Boston and Sid for turning my helmet into a toilet.

PROUD SPONSORS

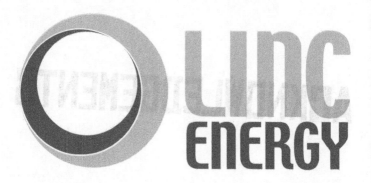

PROUD SPONSORS

PROUD SPONSORS

PROUD SPONSORS